A GRAYWOLF DISCOVERY

Graywolf Discovery books are books we love,
the sort of treasure an enthusiastic reader passes along to friends.
We've discovered some of these ourselves, but most
have been recommended to us by authors, booksellers, or other
members of the family of book-nuts.

The
Estate
of
Poetry

EDWIN MUIR

Foreword by Archibald MacLeish
New Introduction by John Haines

Copyright © 1962 by the President and Fellows of Harvard College

First published by Harvard University Press
Foreword by Archibald MacLeish from the 1962 edition
Introduction copyright © 1993 by John Haines

Publication of this volume is made possible in part by a grant provided by the
Minnesota State Arts Board through an appropriation by the Minnesota State
Legislature, and by a grant from the National Endowment for the Arts.
Additional support has been provided by the Northwest Area Foundation, the
Andrew W. Mellon Foundation, the Lila Wallace-Reader's Digest Fund, the
McKnight Foundation, the Dayton-Hudson Foundation for Dayton's and Target
stores, the Cowles Media Foundation, the General Mills Foundation, and other
generous contributions from foundations, corporations, and individuals.
Graywolf Press is a member agency of United Arts, Saint Paul. To these organi-
zations and individuals who make our work possible, we offer heartfelt thanks.

Published by GRAYWOLF PRESS
2402 University Avenue, Suite 203
Saint Paul, Minnesota 55114.
All rights reserved. Printed in the United States of America.

2   4   6   8   9   7   5   3
First Graywolf Printing, 1993

Library of Congress Cataloging-in-Publication Data
Muir, Edwin. 1887-1959.
The estate of poetry / Edwin Muir:
foreword by Archibald MacLeish: new introduction by John Haines.
p.   cm. -(A Graywolf discovery)
Includes bibliographical references and index.
ISBN 1-55597-182-2
1. Poetry-History and criticism. 2. English poetry-History and criticism.
I. Title II. Series.
809.1-dc20   92-39289

CONTENTS

INTRODUCTION

It is good to have this book in print again. As I recall, I first read *The Estate of Poetry* when I was teaching at the University of Washington in 1974. I was impressed with it then, with its essential decency and its broadness of outlook and I have returned to it many times in the years since. From time to time I have assigned it to graduate classes, and have seldom failed to meet among students a grateful reception for what Muir has to say. Reading him once again, I find in myself renewed respect for the man and his thought.

This is the second of Muir's works that I have been privileged to introduce, the other being *The Story and the Fable*, an early version of his *Autobiography* reprinted by Rowan Tree Press in 1989. That volume particularly, together with the present work, would be enough to assure Muir a lasting reputation even if we did not have his poems. But all of Muir's critical work that I am familiar with can bear rereading, for its intelligence and integrity, even when the immediate occasions for his reviews and essays have passed and become part of the history of literature in our time. Criticism of the kind that Muir wrote, and this can be said of Eliot also, remains active, useful to both poets and readers; it does not date.

In this regard it is well to keep in mind that Muir wrote during the high days of modernism, when the great works were being written or had recently been published and, where necessary, were being translated from other languages. Muir was very much a part of that time with his journalistic work and the translations from Kafka and other European writers undertaken with his wife, Willa. Their translations of Kafka can be said to have established that writer's voice in English, and the Muirs' edition of Hermann Broch's great novel, *The Sleepwalkers*, first published in 1932, is still the standard text.

There have been many studies of poetry in recent years, overwhelmingly aimed at an academic audience, but none so thoughtful, informed, and generous as Muir's. It is particularly useful now to read *The Estate of Poetry* in context with more recent comment on literature and intellectual life. I am thinking, for example, of books like Russell Jacoby's *The Last Intellectuals*, and of Alvin Kernan's *The Death of Literature*. To compare the substance of books like these to Muir–their emphasis on the professionalization of letters and the decline of an independent intellectual life as Muir himself lived it–is to appreciate how much we have lost in the four decades since Muir gave his lectures; how far we have come from a time when a writer of stature might presume to speak to and for the society in which he or she lived, to an attentive and significant audience within it.

I can think of one other text, not widely quoted, that has the seriousness and corresponding absence of self-concern that we find in Muir, and that is Robinson Jeffers' brief essay. "Poetry, Gongorism, and a Thousand Years," published in a limited edition in 1949. However much one might disagree with some of what Jeffers has to say there, expressed as well in his letters and his poems, one does not question the utter honesty and conviction, nor the humane sensibility that lie behind his statements. Poetry for men like Muir and Jeffers, as it was for Wordsworth and for Yeats, had in the end little to do with celebrity and professional cheek, and everything to do with an attitude that, as Muir well knew, lies close to the religious spirit. Those for whom poetry is something more than a career will know what I mean by this.

It is worthwhile, too, to consider *The Estate of Poetry* in the light of Dana Gioia's essay, "Can Poetry Matter?", published last year in the *Atlantic*. Of all recent discussions of poetry and its audience, Gioia's can be said to come closest to Muir in spirit. And by that I mean, among other things, the concern that poetry might one day escape its current institutional dependence and regain, not only a depleted vitality, but something of the authority it once enjoyed in the general life of people.

The *Foreword* contributed to the original edition by Archibald MacLeish and reprinted here, seems to me still to be as admirable an introduction to the man and his work as any that might be written today, and in some respects more in touch with what Muir stood for. I would like merely to reaffirm at this time two or three of the ideas raised by Muir in the course of his lectures.

One of these, already referred to by MacLeish, concerns Muir's emphasis on the tendency of poets to turn inward into poetry and away from society and a potential audience within it. Surely few would now deny that Muir's description has become truer than it was when he wrote; a situation indicative of more than the condition of poetry, and which Octavio Paz has recently likened to the retreat of the arts and intellectual life into the monastery during the Middle Ages.

A second and striking point raised by Muir lies in his remarks on the nature of the poetic forms that have come down to us, and that have in some way become, through repeated and masterly use, organic. Muir's remarks on the subject are among the wisest and least polemical I have read, and of special interest now in view of a contemporary debate concerning *form* as opposed to free verse. We have heard much in our time on the merits and defects of a prevailing habit of verse assumed to speak more directly and adequately to our modern sensibility. Yet there is the alternative possibility suggested by Muir, which I would frame as a question: Is there not, after all, something *organic* in Dante's three-line stanza, whether rhymed or not, something true and eternally useful to poets?

And I would reaffirm one additional idea among Muir's closing remarks, again cited by MacLeish, and that is the idea of a "great theme greatly stated." We forget all too easily, in these days of a diminished public role for poetry, that it is *thought*, the capacity for conceptual thought, together with one's ideal intuition of what the art can be, which allows poetry on occasion to emerge from our all too common private preoccupations into those universal statements that, one can fairly say, compose the art's final justification.

I recommend *The Estate of Poetry* for its wisdom, its clarity and generosity, and for its quiet and embracing passion that offers a balanced and effective reply to all current and perennial wars among poets. What it has to tell us can never grow old, for it is the very ground of poetry.

John Haines
December 1992

✤ ✤ ✤

FOREWORD

Fame, in any generation, is a better guide to the gen-
eration than to its poets — which is why the reputa-
tion of the author of this book is not commensurate with
his accomplishment. Readers of poetry in Edwin Muir's
generation thought of themselves as sophisticated
people, the first English readers since Chaucer's time to
understand that poetry is literature, that literature is
art, that art is European, and that the grandfather of
excellence is therefore Dante, with the line of descent
falling through Provence and Paris to reach the Chan-
nel belatedly about the time of the First World War.
They were uncomfortable in the presence of that other,
older poetry which is at once less and more than litera-
ture and less and more than European, and they re-
gretted its survival into sophisticated, modern times.
Frost, for example, was never one of *the* poets of that

generation. And Edwin Muir, though loved by his friends and respected by everybody, was famous rather as the translator, with his wife Willa, of the novels of Kafka than as one of the authentic poets of the half century: the only poet of the period in whom the crystal eye of poetry was also the limpid eye of innocence.

That curious double vision with its uniquely penetrating power he owed to the happy circumstances of his childhood and the tragedy of his adolescent years. Muir had the poignant fortune, good and bad, of living his first twenty years in two worlds so far apart in historic time that his own life seems almost to recapitulate the history of the social change and industrial revolution which produced the world we live in. The result of that strange fortune was that he brought to the confrontation with chaos, which is the lot of the contemporary mind, a consciousness, a sensibility, which saw farther into his time than any of his contemporaries with the exception of Yeats.

Muir was born into a world as old as Greece and older, a world of farmers who also followed the sea and of fishermen who also farmed. The Orkney Islands off the northeast coast of Scotland were little changed in 1887 from what they had been a thousand years before when they were settled from Norway and Scotland. The language was an old mixture of Norse and Scots and the life, as Muir says in his *Autobiography*, was still the ancient ordered life of the ship and the plow. "The farmers did not know ambition and the petty torments of ambition; they did not know what competition was, though they lived at the end of Queen Victoria's reign; they helped one another with their work when help was required, following the old usage; they had a culture made up of legend, folk-song, and the poetry and prose of the Bible." And elsewhere in that extraordinary book he describes the economy of the farm on the little island of Wyre where he spent his childhood. It was an economy Odysseus would have understood: "Our life at the Bu was virtually self-supporting. The pig, after being slaughtered each year, was cut up and salted, and the pork stored away in a barrel. I helped with the salting when I was quite small, and got a sense of pleased importance from rubbing the raw slices of meat on coarse salt strewn on a wooden board: those neat cubes did not seem to have any connection with the butchered pig. We had fish almost as often as we wanted it, and crabs when Sutherland went to lift his creels; and Aunt Maggie was often down on the beach gathering whelks. The oat bannocks and barley bannocks, the milk, butter, cheese and eggs were our own produce. We sent part of the wool after the sheep-shearing down to a Border town, and it came back as blankets and cloth. We bought at the shop such things as white bread, sugar, tea, treacle, currants and raisins, and paraffin oil for the lamps."

And this life was not only self-supporting in economic terms: it was self-supporting in spiritual terms also. ". . . at the heart of human civilization is the byre, the

barn and the midden. When my father led out the bull
to serve a cow brought by one of our neighbours it was
a ritual act of the tradition in which we have lived for
thousands of years, possessing the obviousness of a long
dream from which there is no awaking. When a neigh-
bour came to stick the pig it was a ceremony as objective
as the rising and setting of the sun." The myth, in other
words, was underneath the furrow and the field in
Orkney, and the limits of reality were not fixed, as they
are with us, by the limits of the probable. "The Orkney
I was born into was a place where there was no great
distinction between the ordinary and the fabulous; the
lives of living men turned into legend. A man I knew
once sailed out in a boat to look for a mermaid, and
claimed afterwards that he had talked with her. . . .
Fairies, or 'fairicks' as they were called, were encoun-
tered dancing on the sands . . ."

What all this would do to the consciousness of a child
one can enviously imagine. Muir's *Autobiography* allows
us to see what it did to a child who was to become a
poet. Writing of the relation of his childhood to his
beginnings as a writer, he recalls a summer afternoon
when a neighboring farmer gave him a lift home from
school in his cart. "He invited me to climb in the back
and I found myself beside a pale young man who smiled
at me and then stared at something which he alone
seemed to see; for he never looked at the fields." This
was the farmer's son "home from Leith." Later that
evening he heard his mother tell his father that the boy

had "come home to die." "The words," says Muir, "were simple and yet strange, and dying became a sad and deliberate act which could be accomplished only in its own place, and for which careful provision had to be made." And the account goes on: "A few weeks later, standing at the end of the house, I watched the funeral procession moving along the distant road. There were six men in front carrying the coffin on their shoulders, and behind them a long line of men in black clothes. Presently they reached the edge of a hill and one by one disappeared. But I stood for a long time afterwards looking at the white empty road, the hills and the sea, and what thoughts were in my mind then I shall never know; they were certainly tinged with sadness, but at the same time suffused with wonder and a simple acceptance of the wonder. The fields were empty out of respect to the dead. It was a calm bright summer day and the hills and the sea hung suspended in light and peace."

At fourteen, by a tragic family miscalculation, that wonder and simple acceptance of wonder were brought face to face with the "modern" world as it revealed itself in the Glasgow of the year 1901. It would scarcely have been possible to take a longer journey. Glasgow, as I saw it a few years later when my father, who had been born there, took his children back, was the most repulsive city of my young experience — and I had started from Chicago. To a child born and brought up on an Orkney farm it should have been a vision of misery. And it was. "I walked to and from my work each day through a slum, for there was no way of getting from the south side of Glasgow to the city except through slums. These journeys filled me with a sense of degradation: the crumbling houses, the twisted faces, the obscene words casually heard in passing, the ancient, haunting stench of pollution and decay, the arrogant women, the mean men, the terrible children, daunted me, and at last filled me with an immense, blind dejection." These terrors and despairs were not imaginary. Within a few years Muir's father, his mother, his brother Willie, and his brother Johnnie were dead — Johnnie of a brain tumor after a terrible illness — and the rest, his two sisters and his brother Jimmie and himself, scattered and lost.

And even then the tragedy was not played out. Muir had his apprenticeship to this industrial, "modern" world to serve and each task was worse than the task before. Underpaid as a clerk in a law office, he became a chauffeur's assistant, then a bookkeeper in a beer-bottling plant, and at last an office hand in a factory for the rendering of bones. "This was a place where fresh and decaying bones, gathered from all over Scotland, were flung into furnaces and reduced to charcoal. The charcoal was sold to refineries to purify sugar; the grease was filled into drums and dispatched for some purpose which I no longer remember. The bones, deco-rated with festoons of slowly writhing, fat yellow mag-gots, lay in the adjoining railway siding, and were shunted into the factory whenever the furnaces were ready for them. . . . Raw, they had a strong, sour penetrating smell. But it was nothing to the stench they gave off when they were shovelled, along with the maggots, into the furnaces. It was a gentle, clinging, sweet stench, suggesting dissolution and hospitals and slaughter-houses, the odour of drains and the rancid stink of bad roasting meat." If Kafka had invented that rancid world he would have been credited with yet another triumph of the grotesque imagination, but not even Kafka could have invented the conjunction of bone factory and Edwin Muir, for Muir was beyond the reach of Kafka's genius.

And yet, it was that conjunction which made the poet. "All that time," Muir wrote, "seemed to give no return, nothing but loss; it was like a heap of dismal rubbish in the middle of which, without rhyme or reason, were scattered four deaths." But there was more than rubbish: there was rubbish framed by the Orkney world — by the furrow and the sea. Fifteen years later, when Glasgow was far behind him and when he had met and married Willa Anderson, the marriage which made possible his life, and when he had served his second apprenticeship, a literary apprenticeship, in London and when, at last, in Germany, he had begun to write poems, he discovered that the furrow and the sea were there — had always been there.

Verse was difficult for him. "I had no training; I was too old to submit myself to contemporary influences; and I had acquired in Scotland a deference toward ideas which made my entrance into poetry difficult." All he could do was blunder along "in baffling ignorance." And then all at once he felt an influence at play, something that moved to help him, and at last he discovered what it was: those years had "come alive after being forgotten so long." The years of his childhood had returned from beyond the rubbish heap and from beyond oblivion to give him what every poet needs, a world in which to hold the world: a stage, he called it — "a symbolical stage on which the drama of human life can play itself out." It was a great gift and he knew how to value it, for he knew that it was not a gift he could have chosen for himself: "I doubt," he said "whether we have the liberty to choose it" — meaning that he doubted whether any poet is free to choose the world he invents. The stage must present *itself*. And it had. "The bare landscape of the little island became, without my knowing it, a universal landscape."

It was that universal landscape which put the heap of rubbish in a right perspective, the perspective in which the heart can see. And it was that perspective which made Edwin Muir the poet he became. He found its metaphor in one of his most famous poems:

One foot in Eden still, I stand
And look across the other land.
The world's great day is growing late,
Yet strange these fields that we have planted
So long with crops of love and hate.
Time's handiworks by time are haunted,

And nothing now can separate
The corn and tares compactly grown.
The armorial weed in stillness bound
About the stalk; these are our own.
Evil and good stand thick around
In the fields of charity and sin
Where we shall lead our harvest in.

Yet still from Eden springs the root
As clean as on the starting day.
Time takes the foliage and the fruit
And burns the archetypal leaf
To shapes of terror and of grief
Scattered along the winter way.
But famished field and blackened tree
Bear flowers in Eden never known.
Blossoms of grief and charity
Bloom in these darkened fields alone.
What had Eden ever to say
Of hope and faith and pity and love
Until was buried all its day
And memory found its treasure trove?
Strange blessings never in Paradise
Fall from these beclouded skies.

One foot in Eden, that "other land" takes on its mean-
ing and its beauty. It is in those darkened fields that
blossoms of grief and charity can bloom. Even Glasgow
is forgiven.

In 1955, a few years before his death, Edwin Muir
came to Harvard to give the Norton lectures. He was a
quiet man with a gentle voice which almost defeated the
public address systems and the engineers, but he was
still the lad Willa Anderson had seen for the first time

almost forty years before, "blue flash in his eyes, charming smile, Nietzsche sticking out of his pocket." Nietzsche was gone by the time he came to us but the surprises were not. American reviewers of his books had prepared the Cambridge audience for a Celt and a mystic, but to the astonishment of everyone Muir devoted his six lectures to an effort "to measure the gap between the public and the poet and to find some explanation why it is so great." Mystics and Celts are not supposed to care about the public or to know that it exists, but here was Muir taking issue with those of his contemporaries who had resigned themselves to the defeated notion that poets write only for other poets and establishing his own position in the great tradition of the Scottish ballads which had a whole nation for audience — not to say a world.

I know no other discussion of this nagging and persistent question as enlightening as Muir's or as courageous, for it takes courage to stand up to the mounted men — those who ride in the saddle of the time. Muir, however, is uncompromising in defining the terms of his dilemma. This "public" of ours, he says, is a new thing under the sun, a faceless aggregation begotten by general education on an artificial, industrial world in which sensibilities have been numbed and imaginations corrupted by the proliferation of those "secondary objects," those machine-made goods, which get between us and experience. When this "public" speaks to us "it speaks indirectly, at intervals, in an ambiguous voice, in newspapers." "It seems to be an impersonal something, a collectivity which, if you break it up, does not reduce itself to a single human being, but at best into chunks of itself, sections, percentages."

That is one side of the great gap. The other is the poet. "What can he say to the public or the public to him?" The language of the public is the language of the "third-party and the on-looker" whereas the poet "is not concerned with life in its generality but in its immediacy and its individuality." His "first allegiance" is to "imaginative truth" and "if he is to serve mankind, that is the only way he can do it." Thus, "the idea of confronting him with the public . . . appears strangely anomalous." But it is made even more anomalous by a temptation which seduces the modern poet and which modern criticism urges on him: "the temptation for poets to turn inward into poetry, to lock themselves into a hygienic prison where they speak only to one another, and to the critic, their stern warder." "The great danger" of the analytic criticism which dominates the time "is that it shuts the poem in upon itself as an object, not of enjoyment but of scrutiny, and cuts it off from the air it should breathe and its spontaneous operation on those who are capable of receiving it."

Seen in this way, the gap between the public and the poet becomes a gap which only the poet can close, and he only by rejecting the temptation of the time. "In the end a poet must create his audience, and to do that he must turn outward." This does not mean that he should attempt to become "a popular poet" for that is no longer possible: "the attempt, if he tried, would only degrade poetry, without being of any profit to the public." But the alternative to popularity is not the academic chrysalis. The alternative is the audience, and this the poet must create for himself as Yeats, who knew that poetry without an audience is inconceivable, created his. But how is an audience to be created? Not by thinking of the public — "its vastness and impersonality would daunt anyone" — but by holding before one's self "the variety of human life, for from that diversity the audience will be drawn."

This is heretical doctrine as Muir well knew. Poets nowadays are not encouraged by their critics to think about audiences, and poems which find audiences of any size — particularly audiences outside the hygienic prison — are deprecated. But heresy did not bother Muir. He saw clearly that "the audience is part of the business" and he understood that "the smaller and more select the audience . . . the more the poet will be confined," which means, conversely, that "the more wide-reaching the imaginative world of poetry . . . the greater will be the audience it wins." Great poetry, he reminds us, was once a general possession of mankind: "a fact which we should not forget — those of us who write poetry, and those of us who criticize it."

It is a fact Edwin Muir never forgot. If anything in our time justifies his hope that "a great theme greatly treated might still put poetry back in its old place" it is his own work.

Archibald MacLeish

Conway, Massachusetts

✢ ✢ ✢

THE ESTATE OF POETRY

THE NATURAL ESTATE

I must begin by explaining what I mean by the estate of poetry. I do not mean the estate over which the poetic imagination rules, whose bounds we do not know. Each individual poet has nothing more than a right of entry to it, and a patch of ground which he is at liberty to cultivate. All sorts and conditions are given that right, men as different as Pope and Blake. You may say that by cultivating his holding each poet adds to the world of poetic imagination, and that therefore it can never be regarded as completely embodied — reason for discouragement and hope, and an earnest of the continuance of poetry. There is a general impression that the entry to this estate has become more difficult, and that once you are in you find the ground is harder to work.

What I mean by the estate of poetry is something simpler: the actual response of a community to the poetry that is written for it; the effective range and influence of poetry. That, as we all know, has greatly shrunk in the last two centuries, and shrunk alarmingly in the century we live in. At present, poetry is neglected in all civilized countries, and it appears to be declining even in what we call uncivilized ones. Poets and lovers of poetry are worried by this, and have been for several decades; and by now their worry has become a settled condition to be accepted with resignation. Sometimes poets are visited by a horrified surprise at the realization that things should be as bad as they are; that their audience has melted away. And for the audience there seems to have been substituted an alarming, vast, shapeless something, deaf and blind to a once recognized and accepted part of life, and a human inheritance. That something is called the public, and it is quite unworried, does not know what it has lost, and goes its way.

The estate of poetry I am mainly concerned with is relatively simple. By that I mean only that if we had enough knowledge we could account for its varying fortunes, say why it flourished at certain times and dwindled in others, and why, to those who still maintain a foothold in it, either as poets or readers, it is becoming more and more a solitary post to be defended against a mysterious and growing encroachment. But we do not have the knowledge we would require for this, for poetry is involved with the historical process which has brought us where we are, and cannot be

separated from it. If the estate has shrunk, if the peas-
antry, or what is left of it, has now no poetry of its
own, and the more leisured classes are also without the
poetry they used to cultivate and enjoy, this has not
come about because of some change in the nature of
poetry, but because of an historical process which has
radically transformed society and the life which it offers
alike to ordinary and extraordinary human beings. We
can pick out certain dry theoretical causes which have
contributed to the recurrent crises of poetry: political and
economic and social changes, intellectual discoveries,
and the inventions of applied science which have altered
the outward lives of peoples. But these do not help us
very much except by assuring us that the changes which
have affected so many of our lives must have affected
poetry too. And it seems to me that the fears of poets
for the future of poetry are merely a part of the general
fear, known so well to all of us, for the future of the
world.

What is palpably clear to us is that the changes, which
have led up to our world as we know it, now govern our
lives. Our very eyes, ears, and noses make us aware of it;
we breathe in a world which would have appeared more
strange to people living a hundred years ago than the
last city built on the foundations of Troy would have
been to those who lived in the first. If we think of
London or New York in the nineties, we realize that
they were quite different cities, except for a few old
buildings incorporated in them, from the cities we call

by their names now; that the houses, the streets, the goods in the shop-windows, the sounds, the smells, are quite different. I imagine the very faces have changed. And all this has been crowded into one lifetime.

Some time ago I came across an old volume of the *Strand Magazine*, with photographs of the London streets of sixty years ago. They showed a quiet, leisurely, almost country-town scene: a few people in odd-looking clothes strolling about, a few hansom cabs, perhaps with Sherlock Holmes in one of them. I did not feel that I was looking at what would nowadays be called a metropolis. We are worried about the acceleration of time, but time is always more rapid than we realize, and the present always seems more natural than the past, simply because our daily lives are spent in it. Only now and then do we know that it has forced on us a new kind of sensibility, imposed new habits and with that new ways of thought, and determined the speed at which we live and feel. These changes, so intimately involved with our lives, are bound to affect our response to literature. Indeed, they may help to explain why we neglect it; we live at such a speed that we are carried straight past it.

The problem is not a new one. In the year 1800, Wordsworth wrote his preface to the second edition of the *Lyrical Ballads*, and what he says then is still true now. He realized that the life of England was changing, and he was troubled by the change. He began by stating his aim as a poet, which was "by fitting to metrical arrangement a selection of the real language of men in a state

4

of vivid sensation," to ascertain how far "that sort of pleasure and that quantity of pleasure may be imparted, which a poet may rationally endeavour to impart." In a striking phrase he adds that his object is to keep the reader "in the company of flesh and blood." Then he goes on:

The human mind is capable of being excited without the application of gross and violent stimulants; and he must have a very faint perception of its beauty and dignity who does not know this, and who does not further know that one being is elevated above another in proportion as he possesses this capability. It has therefore appeared to me that to endeavour to produce or enlarge this capability is one of the best services in which, at any period, a writer can be engaged; but this service, excellent at all times, is especially so at the present day. For a multitude of causes, unknown to former times, are now acting with a combined force to blunt the discriminating powers of the mind, and, unfitting it for all voluntary exertion, to reduce it to a state of almost savage torpor. The most effective of these causes are the great national events which are daily taking place [the Napoleonic Wars] and the increasing accumulation of men in cities [the Industrial Revolution], where the uniformity of their occupations produces a craving for extraordinary incident, which the rapid communication of intelligence hourly gratifies. To this tendency of life and manners the literature and theatrical exhibitions of the country have conformed themselves.

These words throw a light on the present state of poetry which we cannot easily provide ourselves; we have grown too familiar with our world. It does not often occur to us that rapid communication of information blunts the discriminating powers of the mind, and may reduce it to a state of savage torpor. Nor do we see at first glance that this has anything to do with our response to literature. It is good, therefore, that we should remember those effects which already seemed so clear to Wordsworth. The other causes mentioned by him for the blunting of the discriminating powers are well known, and often discussed: the increasing accumulation of men in cities, and the monotony of their occupations there, and the craving for violent stimulants which is provided for now by the gangster film, the horror comic, and murder stories in the newspapers.

Wordsworth speaks next of his position as a poet:

When I think upon this degrading thirst after outrageous stimulation, I am almost ashamed to have spoken of the feeble endeavour made in these volumes to counteract it; and, reflecting upon the magnitude of the general evil, I should be oppressed by no dishonourable melancholy, had I not a deep impression of certain inherent and indestructible qualities of the human mind, and likewise of certain powers in the great and permanent objects that act upon it, which are equally inherent and indestructible; and were there not added to this impression a belief that the time is approaching when the evil will be systematically opposed, by men of greater powers, and with far more distinguished success.

No poet could write like that about poetry now. Wordsworth was wrong in imagining that the evil would be systematically opposed; we know that it could not, for the world, with its full force, was pressing in the opposite direction. The development of society was making life, for the great mass of men, more and more uniform, and it has since made poetry, a few centuries ago known and enjoyed in every peasant community, a thing which is written for the few, while the mass of the people now read the news and go to the cinema, or sit before a television set. The public has become one of the subjects of poetry, but is no longer its audience. Coleridge felt as Wordsworth did when he spoke in the Dejection Ode of

> that inanimate cold world allowed
> To the poor loveless ever-anxious crowd.

A forlorn image of the city. The inherent and inde-structible qualities of the human mind and the great and permanent objects that act upon it remain, though we live in a world of objects which are more and more impermanent.

The world we live in is quite convincing. It has the appearance of being a world: a certain tinsel perma-nence, and a distinctive quality which makes it different from any world in the past. Trying to distinguish it from these other worlds, one sees it more and more as a world of secondary objects, of finished articles. These are immensely convenient for us, and that is the first aspect of them which is likely to impress us; we are aware of their other effects only in uneasy reflection, perhaps as a vague realization that we have lost some-thing, we do not know what. But life may help us by

analogy to understand the decline of imaginative litera-
ture. Two hundred years ago, in the civilization then
natural to man, the farmer grew his own wheat and
corn, ground it at the neighboring mill, killed and cut
up his own pigs and oxen, and lived a poor, coarse, but
self-sufficient life. He knew the value of bread, knowing
how hard and precarious was the work of producing it,
and was careful to look after his horses and cattle be-
cause their labor and their meat were necessary to him.
His valuation of them was therefore a true valuation. In
the same way the craftsman knew the material he fash-
ioned and watched it changing under his hands from
its rough to its finished state. He could tell good work
from bad, and put a value on it. Now that we buy in
shops shoulders of beef, loaves, chairs, beds, pots and
pans, automobiles, and refrigerators, almost everything
that has become necessary or convenient for us, we are
eased of a great deal of labor, and have lost touch with
a world of experience. I am not advocating a return to
a past that has gone forever, or romanticizing the coarse-
ness of peasant life, or its poverty and hardship. All I
want to suggest is that the vast dissemination of second-
ary objects isolates us from the natural world in a way
which is new to mankind, and that this cannot help
affecting our sensibilities and our imagination. It is
possible to write a poem about horses, for, apart from the
work they do for us, they have a life of their own; it is
impossible to write a poem about motor cars, except in
the false rhetorical vein, for they have no life except

what we give them by pushing a starter. The finished article is finished in a final sense; sometimes we can admire its functional beauty, but it is impervious to the imagination. This artificial world which we have made out of the world, the monotony of the work which produces it, the abundance of the distractions which vainly try to make up for that monotony — all these things, it seems to me, help to explain the depressed state of poetry, and the present neglect of it. Poetry flourishes when there is a public with a natural affinity for it.

I shall leave the problem at this point and turn to what may be called the natural estate of poetry, which is also its original estate. No one doubts that poetry was once more widely enjoyed; yet we tend to forget the extent of its province and the variety of its parishes. I can speak of one of them, fortunately, from my own experience. I was brought up in a group of islands on the north of Scotland, remote enough for life there to have remained almost unchanged for two hundred years. In our farmhouse in one of the smaller Orkney islands, there were not many books apart from the Bible, *The Pilgrim's Progress*, and the poems of Burns. Except for Burns we had no poetry books, but we knew a great number of ballads and songs which had been handed down from generation to generation. These, sometimes with the airs traditionally belonging to them, were known in all the farms; there must have been hundreds of them. They were part of our life, all the more because we knew them by heart, and had not acquired but inherited them. They

9

were not contemporary in any sense, but entered our present from the past. The only innovation in our ancestral life was the weekly visit of a little steamer and the weekly arrival of a local newspaper. The newspaper was mere "literature" to us, to be scrutinized almost as a modern critic of the more cautious kind might examine a poem; the songs and ballads were our real unquestioned sustenance and enjoyment. They were almost all Scottish, but, occasionally, perhaps because of the steamer, fashionable songs from London reached us. I remember the first coming of the Victorian hit, "After the Ball was over"; but its vogue did not last for long.

I am trying to describe what poetry meant, all those years ago, to an uncultivated but in a real sense civilized community, a more civilized one than you will easily find now. What did we think of poetry? We did not *think* of it at all. If we had chanced to do that, probably the most we could have said would have been that it was both strange and natural, that it was different from any other kind of speech — but why not? — that the meter and rhyme resembled music, so that poetry appeared to be something halfway between music and speech. If there was any mystery about it, that was a natural mystery, so natural that we would never have thought of questioning it, or have felt any desire to inquire into it.

Now this treasury of poetry had been preserved by many generations of peasants in Orkney, in Scotland and England, and the countries of Europe, for hundreds of years. The fact that it had been preserved shows how much it was prized, and also that poetry was taken to be a natural thing: an exercise of the heart and the imagination. And that is why I call this the natural estate of poetry.

So far as we know, these anonymous songs and ballads rose among the peasantry and were made by them. The authors, if that is what they should be called, knew nothing of poetry except by inheritance. I have heard it suggested that these songs and ballads were created communally, a theory which may have arisen from the fact that they were not only a means of communication, but also a means of participation in something belonging to and shared by everyone. The idea that they were made up by a sort of committee is absurd; one has only to turn to the great ballads to realize how absurd it is. On the other hand, if we can think of their creation in time rather than in space, we realize that there was after all a cooperation in their making, for it is clear from the many versions of them that exist that they were not merely transmitted in a passive way, but modified in their transmission, often to their advantage. It may take hundreds of years to bring a ballad to its perfection, and many generations may participate in its making, and the critical faculty cannot help coming into play.

The critic as we know him did not, of course, exist in the time and the circle I am trying to describe. I fancy that it was not until poetry was written down that formal criticism could come into being. But it would be a mistake to imagine that before this the audience always listened to poetry uncritically. All that was given to the listener, it is true, was the run of the words and the tunes and the rhythms, the changing sequence of a story in the ballad, and the movement of feeling in a song. But the audience for spoken poetry had a more powerful memory than most of us have now. The listener's memory was his book, and he could turn over its leaves as we turn over our printed pages. Particular episodes in a poem, moving expressions of feeling, felicitous lines, would be recalled and repeated by the judicious listener (it is hard to account otherwise for some of the lines in the ballads), these lines would be discussed, excite wonder or praise, and eventually perhaps come to influence the development of spoken poetry — simply through the response to it. But it is misleading even to speak of the poem and the audience, when the audience may be both listening to the poem and shaping it, be both sharing it and transmitting it.

Much of this poetry was in the great style; it embraced tragedy in such ballads as "Clerk Saunders" and "Sir Patrick Spens"; it dealt with the mysterious and the supernatural in "Thomas the Rhymer," "The Daemon Lover," and "The Wife of Usher's Well"; it took in comedy in some of the songs and in ballads like "The Barring o' oor Door." But its note was mainly tragic, without a single note of didactic comment: all was passion and the tragic outcome of passion, set down in the barest words. The style of this poetry, especially in the ballads, is not popular in the accepted sense, that is, the style which a writer more intelligent than his audience adopts when he tries to make clear to them things which are not clear in themselves. The ballads are not popular but traditional; and they were born out of a tradition so ancient and so indisputable that it required no explanation, and had passed beyond opinion. So that you will never find in them those observations on human life which make the poetry of Burns so attractive and so popular. They are in a different world from the world in which "A man's a man for a' that," or where we are moved by reflections such as that

> The hert's aye
> The pairt aye
> That mak's us richt or wrang,

or that

> The best laid schemes o' mice and men
> Gang aft a-gley.

The ballads are, with respect to Burns, on a different level; the level of tragic acceptance. They are equally far from the world of the insulted and injured which tortured Dostoevsky's imagination. They lie on the other side of the great plateau of the eighteenth century, with its humanitarian passion and its vast hopes for mankind. And the early tragic world which they summon up was the poetic sustenance of the peasantry for hundreds of years.

This poetry has no sentimental appeal. It simply sets down life as it appeared to the peasantry: an ancestral vision simplified to the last degree. And this extreme simplification molded its style into an instrument of the communal imagination. That style is immediately recognizable and is indisputable as the style of a great poet. Its marks are brevity and strength. It plunges straight into the theme:

> Clerk Saunders and May Margaret
>   Walk'd owre yon garden green;
> And deep and heavy was the love
>   That fell thir twa between,

or

> Yestreen the Queen had four Maries,
>   The night she'll hae but three,

or

> The king sits in Dunfermline town
>   Drinking the blude-red wine.

Its passion is sometimes touched with a sardonic irony. When the Daemon Lover is asked by his deluded sweetheart where he is taking her in his ship, he says

> I'll show where the white lilies grow
>   On the banks o' Italie,

an alluring and magical image. But when the storm rises and she sees his cloven hoof, she asks again and he answers,

> I'll show where the white lilies grow,
>   In the bottom o' the sea.

14

Except for those which are concerned with legendary or supernatural subjects, most of the ballads deal with actual events. "Sir Patrick Spens" describes a historical incident. A ship was sent out in winter to bring a Norwegian princess to Scotland to marry a Scottish king. On the way back the ship was wrecked, and the princess and the Scottish lords who had gone to escort her were drowned. When, long after this, Walter Scott and James Hogg were going about the Scottish Borders persuading old women to sing or intone the old poetry, people no longer knew the occasion of the ballad. History had been transmuted into poetry, and only the poetry was left. Hogg's mother told him that he was doing wrong in writing down the ballads, and that the printed page would kill them. And it did help to kill a characteristic mode of perpetuating poetry, and the communal participation which had kept it alive. The ballads, printed, no longer belonged to the peasantry. You will not find many ballads current among what is left of them now, nor any of much value that have been made since. What Wordsworth dreaded so much, the rapid communication of information, debased the very subject matter of that kind of poetry. In the poorer parts of the industrial towns in Scotland a few ballads still survive in a degenerate form as children's songs, pathetically brought down-to-date, with a paraphernalia of gangsters and molls and machine guns. But in these new versions the poetry has quite disappeared.

The action of the old ballads was tragic, but it took

15

place in a world where the supernatural might appear at any moment. The three dead sons of the wife of Usher's Well come back about the Martinmas time, when the nights are lang and mirk: and their hats are of the birk. They return on the night when souls are supposed to be released from Purgatory. The birch leaves on their hats grow on the banks of Paradise. Here the legend is a Christian one; but in other ballads it is partly Christian and partly Pagan, and includes Heaven, Hell and Elfland. Three verses in the ballad of "Thomas the Rhymer" give a geographical chart of that supernatural landscape. Thomas meets on earth a lady so beautiful that he salutes her as the Queen of Heaven; she answers that she is the Queen of Elfland, and that he must go with her. Then she shows him the three roads:

> O see ye not yon narrow road,
>   So thick beset wi' thorns and briars?
> That is the Path of Righteousness,
>   Though after it but few inquires.
>
> And see ye not yon braid, braid road,
>   That lies across the lily leven?
> That is the Path of Wickedness,
>   Though some call it the Road to Heaven.
>
> And see ye not yon bonny road
>   That winds about the fernie brae?
> That is the Road to fair Elfland
>   Where thou and I this night maun gae.

To reach Elfland they have to take a fabulous journey:

O they rade on and farther on,
  And they waded rivers abune the knee;
And they saw neither sun nor mune,
  But they heard the roaring of the sea.

There is no return from the heavenly or the hellish road; but, after seven years in Elfland, True Thomas comes back to the earth.

This supernatural world embodied for the peasantry their sense of the mystery surrounding them, in which they saw at one glance and with no sense of incongruity, Christian revelation and natural magic. There is a strange poem, called by some a fairy's song and by others a ghost's song, and it gives better than any other an idea of the strength and realism of peasant belief in the land of faerie and its intercourse with the human world. I have been told that it comes from Northumberland, on the English side of the Border;

Wae's me, wae's me,
The acorn's not yet
Fallen from the tree
That's to grow the wood
That's to make the cradle
That's to rock the bairn
That's to grow a man
That's to lay me.

At first glance this song looks like a riddling children's rhyme; but the more one reads it the uncannier it becomes. The acorn has still to fall, the tree has still to grow and be cut down, the cradle is still to make, the child to be born and become a man: an unimaginable stretch of time, and at the end of it a certain event, a far-distant death. To lay a ghost is to give it peace; to lay a body is to prepare it for burial. Because it begins as a lamentation, I incline to the fairy's song rather than the ghost's. We have it on the authority of Yeats that the fairies are old, old and gay; but they are not immortal. The belief in Elfland must have been very firm and exactly formulated before anyone could have written that song. And the belief was supported by local knowledge; people knew the places where the fairies lived. You can still see the hill in the border country under which True Thomas lived with the Queen of Elfland for seven years.

I have tried to describe the world of imagination in which the ballads lived; I cannot leave them without saying something of the rude yet sometimes extraordinarily felicitous art which shaped them. Their economy, especially in the dramatic employment of dialogue, is what strikes one first, and after that their use of tragic irony. One could illustrate this last quality from a score of ballads, but perhaps the best examples are to be found in "Sir Patrick Spens." The magnificent opening lines,

> The king sits in Dunfermline town
> Drinking the blude-red wine,

stand in ironic contrast to all the dark action that follows. But the irony comes out explicitly when the ship is foundering:

O laith, laith were our gude Scots lords
  To wet their cork-heel'd shoon,
But lang or a' the play was play'd
  They wat their hats aboon.

At the end comes one of those inspired expansions of the
theme which delight us in great art. The balladist has
seen the action, the storm gathering, the ship sinking,
and nothing but that; then come the lines, filled with a
different and tender irony:

O lang, lang may the ladies sit,
  Wi' their fans into their hand,
Before they see Sir Patrick Spens
  Come sailing to the strand.

And lang, lang may the maidens sit
  Wi' their gowd kames in their hair,
A'waiting for their ain dear loves,
  For them they'll see nae mair.

Half-owre, half-owre to Aberdour,
  'Tis fifty fathoms deep,
And there lies gude Sir Patrick Spens,
  Wi' the Scots lords at his feet.

It is an exquisite touch to bring in the maidens and the
ladies, and the fans and the gold combs, after the dark-
ness of the storm. The handling of color and ornament
in the ballads is very striking. Generally they are used
as images of the natural, sensuous life which lies outside
the tragic action, or which has been destroyed by it. The
color of the ballads is dark, and in that atmosphere the
simplest evocation of color or luxury has an intense

brightness. To show how effective these touches are, here is the shortest version of one of the ballads, the lament of a woman who had been deserted by her lover:

O waly, waly, up the bank,
    And waly, waly, doun the brae,
And waly, waly, yon burn-side,
    Where I and my Love wont to gae.
I lean'd my back unto an aik,
    I thocht it was a trustie tree;
But first it bow'd and syne it brak —
    Sae my true love did lichtlie me.

O waly, waly, gin love be bonnie
    A little time while it is new!
But when 'tis auld it waxeth cauld,
    And fades awa' like morning dew.
When we cam in by Glasgow toun,
    We were a comely sicht to see;
My Love was clad in the black velvèt,
    And I mysell in cramasie.

But had I wist before I kist'
    That love had been sae ill to win,
I had lock'd my hert in a case o' gowd,
    And pinn'd it wi' a siller pin.
And O! if my young babe were born,
    And set upon the nurse's knee,
And I mysell were dead and gane,
    And the green grass growing over me.

How clearly the images of color and luxury stand there for what has been lost, and for what might have been: the black velvet and the crimson dress representing past happiness; and the case of gold and silver pin the innocence of heart which has been lost, so precious that only the most rare substances were fit to guard it. I do not know whether the art of this ballad was purely instinctive; we do not know how far any great poetry is instinctive and how far consciously shaped. The Queen of Elfland lives beyond the reach of care, and so it is right that

> Her skirt was o' the grass-green silk,
>   Her mantel o' the velvet fyne;
> At ilka tett o' her horse's mane,
>   Hung fifty siller bells and nine.

But, in the ballad of "The Twa Sisters," the images of beauty and luxury come only after the elder one has pushed the younger into the river, and she has drowned. The miller's son runs out and calls to his father to draw the dam, crying

> Here's either a mermaid or a swan.

And then:

> You coudna see her yallow hair
> For gold and pearle that were so rare.

> You coudna see her middle sma'
> For gouden girdle that was sae braw.

A minstrel comes by, and takes three locks of her yellow hair, and strings his harp with them. And first he sings to the harp, "Farewell to my father the king," and then "Farewell to my mother the queen," and last, "Wae to my sister, fair Ellen."

This then was the sustenance on which for hundreds of years the peasantry lived; on this they formed their imaginative idea of human life. I say hundreds of years, but perhaps I should have said ages rather than centuries. For who knows when poetry began? It may be that a much older poetry breathed itself out in the ballads; a poetry that had existed long before Homer.

There is a greater poetry than that of the ballads; they do not contain those universal statements of life which we find in Dante and Shakespeare; but they were once a general possession as Shakespeare has never been. And that great poetry can, or once could, be a general possession is a fact which we should not forget: those of us who write poetry, and those of us who criticize it. If we could keep it in mind, I think it would give us a more just and adequate idea of poetry.

＊ ＊ ＊

WORDSWORTH:
RETURN TO THE SOURCES

I return to the distinction between the imaginative
realm of poetry, and its worldly good or bad fortune,
its possession of a large or small audience. These two
estates can be considered separately, but not for long. For
it is clear that the more wide-reaching the imagina-
tive world of poetry is, the greater will be the audience
it wins. Or the case can be put conversely. The smaller
and more select the audience for poetry, the more the
poet will be confined. The smallness of the audience can-
not but discourage him, and in doing that diminish his
imaginative scope: all this no doubt within limits.
Those who now write poetry know that they are writing
for a few, since few people will read them, and this
must influence without their knowing it the poetry that
they write. I do not mean that contemporary poets sacri-

23

fice their integrity for the shadow of a select reputation, or that when they are conceiving their poems they ever think of the audience. But they are aware of what is possible, given their small audience, and what is not. They know that they write in a tiny, on the whole benevolent, vacuum, through which no warmth from the great world outside penetrates, whereas in happier ages the sustaining warmth, the atmosphere of expectation, was there.

Before I leave oral poetry, I mean to give one more example of the effect which an immediate and communal response to poetry can produce. It is from a dialogue of Plato, "Ion: or on the Iliad." In this dialogue Socrates draws out a young rhapsodist who went from city to city in Greece declaiming Homer. It was an age when poetry was still known mainly as a thing spoken; the tragedies of Aeschylus and Sophocles and the epics of Homer were heard by tens of thousands, but were otherwise accessible to very few. Ion, Socrates' interlocutor, was famous throughout all Greece as a rhapsodist, and was regarded as matchless in his interpretations of Homer. Socrates begins by asking him whether he excels in interpreting Homer alone, or whether he is equally good in reciting Hesiod. Ion replies that when any other poet than Homer is mentioned he cannot listen, and simply goes to sleep. Socrates leads him on from point to point, and at last convinces him that he does not understand the art he is so proud of, or even know what he is saying. Then comes the point toward which Socrates has been leading; and it is that Ion does not declaim Homer, as he thinks, according to art and knowledge, but by inspiration.

For the authors of those great poems which we admire, do not attain to excellence through the rules of any art, but they utter their beautiful melodies of verse in a state of inspiration, and, as it were, *possessed* by a spirit not their own. Thus the composers of lyrical poetry create those admired songs of theirs in a spirit of divine insanity, like the Corybantes, who lose all control over their reason in the enthusiasm of the sacred dance, and, during this supernatural possession, are excited to the rhythm and harmony which they communicate to men. . . . For a poet is indeed a thing ethereally light, winged, and sacred, nor can he compose anything worth calling poetry until he becomes inspired and, as it were, mad, or whilst any reason remains in him. For while a man retains any portion of the thing called reason, he is utterly incompetent to produce poetry. In other respects poets may be sufficiently ignorant and incapable.

To many of us these may seem wild and whirling words, and we may feel inclined to read into them the Socratic irony, and there may indeed have been a small but not deadly dose of it there. But we must remember that Socrates was considering poetry from the point of view of a philosopher, and examining it strictly from that point of view. How could he find reason in such a strange thing? And, failing to find reason there, what was left for him to apprehend but a peculiar kind of madness which he had to call divine, since, in spite of his own devotion to reason, he was carried away by it? He had brought Ion to this point by a rigorous argument. He had asked him:

When you declaim well, and strike your audience with admiration, whether you sing of Odysseus rushing upon the threshold of his palace, discovering himself to the suitors, and pouring his shafts out at his feet; or of Achilles assailing Hector; or of those affecting passages concerning Andromache, or Hecuba, or Priam, are you then self-possessed? or rather, are you not rapt and filled with such enthusiasm for the deeds you recite, that you fancy yourself in Ithaca or Troy, or wherever else the poem transports you?

Ion confesses:

You speak most truly, Socrates, nor will I deny it; for when I recite of sorrow my eyes fill with tears; and when of fearful and terrible deeds my hair stands on end, and my heart beats fast.

Then Socrates asks:

Tell me, Ion, can we call him in his senses, who weeps while dressed in splendid garments, and crowned with a golden coronal, not losing any of these things? and is filled with fear when surrounded by ten thousand friendly persons, not one of whom desires to despoil or injure him? Do you often perceive your audience moved too?

Ion replies:

Many among them, and frequently. I, standing on the rostrum, see them weeping, with eyes fixed earnestly on me, and overcome by my declamation.

After many centuries of criticism, this dialogue may seem extraordinarily simple, both in its questions and its answers. Yet I think it tells us something about poetry. I do not mean the passage where Socrates questions the value of art, and denies that poetry is at all a conscious or understandable thing. We know that the poet does attain part, sometimes the chief part of his excellence, by the rules of art, and that poetry, if conceived in a state of inspiration, or divine madness, or possession, is not born except with the assistance of art. Where Socrates does tell us something about poetry is when he inquires into Ion's state when he is reciting Homer, and the response he awakens in the ten thousand friendly persons. How account on any reasonable grounds for the tears and the painful beating of the heart?

I remember many years ago sitting in a restaurant in London with a Spanish writer. In a hall over the way there was a dancing floor, and we could see the heads of the dancers only, bobbing apparently to ragtime music. These heads looked quite ridiculous. The Spanish writer, who detested Bernard Shaw for what he thought his shallow rationalism, said: "That is how Shaw sees poetry." And to Socrates the philosopher, if he had not felt the power of poetry, the spectacle of a multitude of adult people weeping together over the imaginary presentation of things long past and far distant might easily have appeared as ridiculous as those bobbing heads — difficult to account for as the result of deliberate art or knowledge. Hamlet asks the same question, after listening to the poor player bursting his heart over the sorrows of the mobled queen:

What's Hecuba to him or he to Hecuba?

And why should the death of Sir Patrick Spens and the Scottish lords have been lamented for hundreds of years in the cottar houses of the Scottish peasantry?

The answer one would be most likely to give now is that the ten thousand friendly persons were moved by Homer's art as interpreted by Ion. And that is true; but it looks at the poetry only, and leaves out the audience who are participating in it. And the audience is part of the business, though we nowadays are disposed to ignore it, knowing that its part has become so small. Why should the ten thousand mourn for the fortunes of men and women dead long ago unless it was themselves and life and time that they mourned for? Yet for them to grieve even over such things, in a sort of supernumerary grief by which in a sense they were comforted, was not an act that could be accounted for or approved by pure reason, and it does not refute, but rather endorses Socrates' claim that poetry is a divine madness. The collective mourning gives a more adequate idea of the original nature of poetry than we have had ever since poetry has been understood more and more strictly as an art. The immediate participation of the audience in the poetry makes the strangeness of the poetic experience immediate and palpable, and restores to it something which it has lacked, except in dramatic tragedy, perhaps ever since the invention of printing.

The emotions that Ion describes were evoked by the recounting of an action, a story. An ode or a song could not have affected an audience in the same way; the emotion would have been more purely pleasurable and less overwhelming, unless it referred to some tragic event known to everyone. The tragic story affects us with unique power because it moves in time, and because we live in time. It reminds us of the pattern of our lives; and within that pattern it brings our loves, our passions, their effects, and unavoidable chance. Matthew Arnold urged that the representation of an action was essential for a great poem, and he may have meant something like this, since a story gives a more complete idea of our temporal lives than any other means that has been discovered. But with the disappearance of the greater audience the story has declined; some poets of our time have used it effectively: I think of Robert Frost and certain poems of T. S. Eliot. But the story, although it is our story, is disappearing from poetry.

It has been taken over by the novel, but expanded there into something quite unlike what it was when used in poetry. The old story was quite simple. It followed some figure — Odysseus, or Ruth, or King David — through time; and it remains the most pure image that we have of temporal life, tracing the journey which we shall take. The novel also tells a story in time, but it is almost as concerned with the relations which space imposes upon us; it deals, at its most typical, with society. It gives us a description or a report, not a clear image of life. The story conceived in this way is of very little use to poetry, and I cannot think of any instance in which it has been successfully used there. But the story in time was once one of the main resources of poetry, and it will be used again, if only because we lose so much by losing it.

This is the problem that troubled Wordsworth. In his *Lyrical Ballads* preface, in which he sets out his aim as a poet, he explains:

The principal object . . . proposed in these poems was to choose incidents and situations from common life, and to relate or describe them, throughout, as far as was possible in a selection of language really used by men, and, at the same time, to throw over them a certain colouring of imagination, whereby ordinary things should be presented to the mind in an unusual aspect; and further, and above all, to make these incidents and situations interesting by tracing in them, truly though not ostentatiously, the primary laws of our nature.

His aim was to deal with common actions or incidents which involve a story, and the poems in the *Lyrical Ballads* where he carried it out were regarded by him as an experiment. Coleridge, with whom he had often discussed the idea, and who had contributed "The Rime of the Ancient Mariner" to the collection, used the same term. He and Wordsworth were engaged in a common experiment: a word which was much used again in the first three decades of this century. But the conscious aims of a poet, no matter how admirable, may not chime with his genius. Wordsworth did write some very fine poems dealing with "incidents and situations from common life." Among them are that great poem, "The Affliction of Margaret — ," and, in a different manner, "Resolution and Independence," and "Michael," and all the Matthew poems. And, while he was writing "The Prelude," he showed again and again his fascination with incident and situation. But, except in a few poems of which "The Affliction of Margaret — " is the greatest, he seldom was content to tell the story simply as a story, was seldom disinterested as the makers of the ballads were. Perhaps he was too concerned with tracing "the primary laws of our being," a task which did not trouble Homer or the ballad-makers; and he did not always trace them unostentatiously. "Resolution and Independence" is a great poem, and we draw genuine comfort from it, as we are intended to do. But it is not on the same level as "The Affliction of Margaret—," which does not try to comfort us at all.

The Margaret of the poem, it is told, was an old lady who kept a little shop in the town of Penrith in Cumberland. Her son had left her to seek his fortunes abroad, and she had never heard from him after. As a boy Wordsworth had known her, and remembered how she would rush out into the street and look wildly about her, hoping that she would catch sight of her son at last. The great virtues of the poem are its sustained imagination and the inevitability of its development.

> To have despaired, have hoped, believed,
> And been forevermore beguiled;
> Sometimes with thoughts of very bliss!

I catch at them, and then I miss;
Was ever darkness like to this?

How wonderfully moving is the line

Sometimes with thoughts of very bliss,

evoking those moments of delusive joy which intervene
in a long contest between hope and despair
Her fears for her son have grown into a vision of the
unknown places of the earth, for he may be in any of
them:

Perhaps some dungeon hears thee groan,
Maimed, mangled by inhuman men;
Or thou upon a desert thrown
Inheritest the lion's den;
Or hast been summoned to the deep,
Thou, thou and all thy mates, to keep
An incommunicable sleep.

The knowledge even that he is dead would be a relief
from the anguish of uncertainty:

I look for ghosts; but none will force
Their way to me: 'tis falsely said
That there was ever intercourse
Between the living and the dead;
For, surely, then I should have sight
Of him I wait for day and night,
With love and longings infinite.

Her fears are communicated to the most harmless
things:

My apprehensions come in crowds;
I dread the rustling of the grass;
The very shadows of the clouds
Have power to shake me as they pass.

She reflects finally that her grief cannot be communicated to anyone, and that, though her neighbors feel sorry for her, they cannot understand:

Beyond participation lie
My troubles, and beyond relief:
If any chance to heave a sigh,
They pity me, and not my grief.

The poem employs the plainest language, except where it evokes the vastness of the world where Margaret's son is lost to her.

Or hast been summoned to the deep,
Thou, thou and all thy mates, to keep
An incommunicable sleep,

is not "a selection of language really used by men." Wordsworth here was obeying a law more powerful than the regulations he laid down for himself in his preface. What makes this poem so impressive is the sustained imagination which follows Margaret's most secret alternations of hope and fear; we are in her mind from beginning to end. Wordsworth's imagination works as strongly in the plainest as in the most beautiful lines. There is no doubt that he could handle an action, a story, and handle it magnificently.

But he had also something else to do, for which he did

not provide in his preface. Among the *Lyrical Ballads* are the "Lines composed a few miles above Tintern Abbey." In them he turns to a compulsive vision of the earth which had come to him as a boy, and again in his youth, and now once more in his twenty-eighth year. He enumerates the blessings which the "beauteous forms" of the Wye valley, revisited after five years, bring him, and among them is

> that blessed mood,
> In which the burthen of the mystery,
> In which the heavy and the weary weight
> Of all this unintelligible world,
> Is lightened: — that serene and blessed mood,
> In which the affections gently lead us on, —
> Until, the breath of this corporeal frame
> And even the motion of our human blood
> Almost suspended, we are laid asleep
> In body, and become a living soul:
> While with an eye made quiet by the power
> Of harmony, and the deep power of joy,
> We see into the life of things.

What Wordsworth is describing is both a physical state and a vision which only in that state was given to him. He lost the vision, as we know, and yet went on writing, for his will was as obstinate as Coleridge's was weak. The sad legacy of his persistence can be found in the ecclesiastical sonnets and the sonnets on capital punishment, and a host of miscellaneous verses. Yet memory, when his mind was compulsively drawn to the past, once or twice renewed the old inspiration. When he heard that James Hogg was dead, his old friendship with Coleridge returned. He was then sixty-five, and his lines on Coleridge are very moving, when we remember that the two friends had been estranged and only imperfectly reconciled:

> Nor has the rolling year twice measured,
> From sign to sign its steadfast course,
> Since every mortal power of Coleridge
> Was frozen at its marvellous source:

> The rapt One of the godlike forehead,
> The heaven-eyed creature sleeps in earth:
> And Lamb, the frolic and the gentle,
> Has vanished from his lonely hearth.

> Like clouds that rake the mountain-summits,
> Or waves that own no curbing hand,
> How fast has brother followed brother,
> From sunshine to the sunless land!

The enchantment which he had shared with Coleridge when they were young was brought back when he realized that Coleridge was dead and the enchantment along with him.

Wordsworth returned to a source of poetry when he returned to incidents and situations of common life; but his return took him farther back; it took him back to the earth itself. He knew with unique clearness that we depend on the earth for our life. This is a common fact; but Wordsworth was aware as no other poet has been of the countless less palpable gifts which we owe to the earth, or to nature. His knowledge came to him, as we

35

have seen, in that blessed mood when we see into the life of things. He was naturally concerned, therefore, with the mood as well as the truth which it brought him. It was for him the poetic mood; and "The Prelude," his autobiography, is a poem about poetry, and the truth which is revealed by it. Sometimes he is more possessed by the mood than by what it tells him about nature and human life. In "Tintern Abbey" he does make a concession to the condition of common life:

> For I have learned
> To look on nature, not as in the hour
> Of thoughtless youth; but hearing oftentimes
> The still, sad music of humanity,
> Nor harsh nor grating, though of ample power
> To chasten and subdue.

We are far here from "The Affliction of Margaret — ," whose grief we cannot reconcile to ourselves so easily. And, having mentioned the still, sad music of humanity, he is carried straight into the other vision which possessed him:

> And I have felt
> A presence that disturbs me with the joy
> Of elevated thoughts; a sense sublime
> Of something far more deeply interfused,
> Whose dwelling is the light of setting suns,
> And the round ocean and the living air,
> And the blue sky, and in the mind of man:
> A motion and a spirit, that impels
> All thinking things, all objects of all thought,
> And rolls through all things.

I think that if Socrates' ten thousand friendly persons had listened to those lines they would have been moved to awe, though not to tears as they were by Homer. They would have felt the presence of divinity.

But that exaltation was to fade into the light of common day. In the Immortality Ode, which was a celebration and perhaps a farewell to his vision, he says:

> The things which I have seen I now can see no more.

He recounts the lovely objects which should make him glad, yet which do not:

> The rainbow comes and goes,
> And lovely is the rose;
> The moon doth with delight
> Look round her when the heavens are bare;
> Waters on a starry night
> Are beautiful and fair;
> The sunshine is a glorious birth;
> But yet I know, where'er I go,
> That there hath pass'd away a glory from the earth.

The vision of the spirit that rolls through all things is fading; he tries to retain it and at the same time to find a comfort in its going. After reverting to

> Delight and liberty, the simple creed
> Of childhood,

he turns upon himself and says,

> Not for these I raise
> The song of thanks and praise;
> But for those obstinate questionings

Of sense and outward things,
Fallings from us, vanishings;
  Blank misgivings of a Creature
Moving about in worlds not realized,
High instincts before which our mortal Nature
Did tremble like a guilty thing surprised.

We feel that his imagination has been humanized, and that he has found that resignation which is a form of acceptance. Another poet might have been led back to incidents and situations of imperfect human life, after this demonstration of the temporal imperfection of his vision. He said in another poem:

A deep despair hath humanised my soul.

Yet, instead of turning to the human scene, he went back to the hills and valleys which had first nourished his vision, but would not nourish it much longer.

The most quintessential of Wordsworth's poetry is not, I think, in the great passages, but in those where he evokes, in some incident, the almost indefinable yet powerful influences which nature exerts on us. We find it in the short poem, "Three years she grew in sun and shower," where nature speaks to her child:

The stars of midnight shall be dear
To her; and she shall lean her ear
  In many a secret place
Where rivulets dance their wayward round,
And beauty born of murmuring sound
  Shall pass into her face.

This exquisite discrimination among things where another poet would be aware of nothing is one of the great virtues of Wordsworth's poetry. The hidden impulses from nature are not always as benign as this. She can warn and inspire fear, but to him the fear too is good. In "The Prelude," speaking of his childhood, he says:

> Fair seed-time had my soul, and I grew up
> Fostered alike by beauty and by fear.

And in the same poem he tells how guilt changed for him the face of nature. As a boy, climbing among the hills, he was tempted to steal a bird caught in another boy's snare:

> And when the deed was done
> I heard among the solitary hills
> Low breathings coming after me, and sounds
> Of undistinguishable motion, steps
> Almost as silent as the turf they trod.

Another time he was climbing a rock-face, on a day of high wind, looking for a raven's nest:

> almost (so it seemed)
> Suspended by the blast which blew amain,
> Shouldering the naked crag, oh, at that time
> While on the perilous ridge I hung alone,
> With what strange utterance did the loud dry wind
> Blow through my ear! the sky seemed not a sky
> Of earth — and with what motion moved the clouds!

His vision of nature becomes more palpable, illustrated by such incidents as these. The passages I have quoted are well known, but they describe best the hallucinatory vividness of Wordsworth's early impressions of nature, and the aftereffects they left with him.

He remembered having these impressions when he was a child of five. He tells how he

> would stand
> Beneath some rock, listening to notes that are
> The ghostly language of the ancient earth,
> Or make their dim abode in distant winds.

And he conversed then, he says,

> With things that really are.

In the long poem, On Man, on Nature, and on Human Life, which he never wrote, these recurrent visions were to be related to universal experience. The poem was to embrace the heaven of heavens, and humanity piping solitary anguish, barricaded evermore within the walls of cities, and the affections which bind us to nature and nature to us. His powers failed before he could achieve his task, and what is left is the great autobiographical poem, "The Prelude," designed to be a preparation for the work, and "The Excursion," in which we see his imagination already shrinking, and his opinions hardening. His central theme was the primal impulse which binds man to nature, and the powers flowing from nature which give more abundant life to man, and the motion of the spirit which rolls through all things. As he grew older nature took on a greater and greater importance; he had confessed in "Tintern Abbey" that nature was once "all in all" to him; now it possessed him again too exclusively; the balance was lost. He who had found love "in huts where poor men lie," had more and more difficulty in dealing with the impulses which bind human beings together. He had once been possessed by an overwhelming vision, and it swept away the admirable intentions with which he started. One can hardly think of a greater contrast than that between the poet as he outlines his program in the preface, and the poet as he is displayed in "The Prelude." I think that Socrates would have found another argument for his claim that poetry is a divine madness, if he could have read those two counter testimonies.

W. B. YEATS

The development of Yeats as a poet is an astonishing spectacle. Midway in it there is a crisis, and after that he becomes a different poet, with other themes, and another voice. Nietzsche once said of Wagner that he was a musician who had made himself into a musician. Yeats was a poet who made himself into a different poet, and a great one.

But, at the start, while he was a boy and a young man, and for a long time after, he seemed to drift on a stagnant stream, waiting for any current or eddy to carry him in the direction where he would find what he was born for. His father being a painter, Yeats for a little while studied painting; but that was not what he wanted. His father admired Darwin and Tyndall, and at first Yeats was a hesitating disciple, but then he violently rejected Darwin and Tyndall. When he went to Trinity College he met a few young men who were writing poetry, and he began to write poetry in a sleepwalking state from which he did not awaken for years. He was concerned then with poetry as an art, the influence of his father, the artist, suggesting to him that art was the greatest of things. In the first poem in his first collection of verse, published when he was twenty-four, these lines occur:

> But O, sick children of the world,
> Of all the many changing things
> In dreary dancing past us whirled,
> To the cracked tune that Chronos sings,
> Words alone are certain good.

AE. had started a hermetic circle in Dublin, and young Yeats was drawn into it, and was soon possessed by the desire for a secret knowledge not to be found in the usual places: a desire which recurred all his life. In London, while attending the meetings of the Rhymers' Club, he was impressed by the fine air and universal knowledge of Lionel Johnson, and began to acquire the air while stopping short of the knowledge. He returned instead to the kind of wisdom which he had sipped at in AE.'s hermetic circle, hoping to gain from it what he needed. His inquiries took him to Madame Blavatsky, the prophetess of theosophy, by whom he was impressed, and to a man of ambiguous character, MacGregor Mathers, who for a time became his friend. He began to practice magic, perhaps because it gave him the feeling of power which he needed, or because he was looking for the special knowledge that would nourish his poetry.

While this was going on Maud Gonne paid a visit to the Yeats house in London. Yeats never forgot his first impression of her: tall and beautiful as a goddess, intrepid and passionate, her heart filled with Irish politics. He fell in love with her at first sight, and thought of her as a reincarnation of Helen of Troy. He tried to influence her and interest her in literary things; but her will was stronger than his, and it plunged him for years into the bitter verbal wars of the Irish Republicans. When he became ill with longing and disappointment, Lady Gregory befriended him. He stayed every now and then in her country house at Coole, and she tried to distract him from his dejection and improve his physical health by taking him round the cottar houses on her estate to listen to the stories of the peasants, filled with supernatural happenings. From her and the life of Coole and the peasantry on the estate he drew the image of life which stayed with him ever after: the pattern of the aristocrat, the poet, and the peasant, which to him made up the good society, and seemed to be the traditional pattern of Irish life. Lady Gregory had also formed the idea of setting up an Irish theater. Yeats had often dreamed of it; now under her influence it became a reality, and he was involved for years in the practical problems, the intrigues and counter-intrigues, inseparable from such work. He found to his surprise that he had the gifts needed for it; he learned to be politic with committees, and became an excellent public speaker and a different man. He had encountered opposition from Maud Gonne and could do nothing against it; he now encountered a different kind of opposition and found he could deal with it. There have been explanations of Yeats in plenty, and I have no wish to add to them, for I feel that to explain anyone is an attempt that should never be made. I am concerned with the poetry, and what worked such a radical change in it, and the probable forces in Yeats's life which may have helped to bring the change about. It seems clear that he must have learned something at least about human nature, something not entirely to his liking, during his campaign for the Abbey Theatre and his attempts to educate the Irish public, something which eventually changed his poetry, giving it hardness and eloquence.

That extraordinary early passivity of Yeats, that almost hypnotic susceptibility, lasted until he was over thirty and had started to be a man of action.

"Your eyes that once were never weary of mine
Are bowed in sorrow under pendulous lids,
Because our love is waning."
                    And then she:
"Although our love is waning, let us stand
By the lone border of the lake once more,
Together in that hour of gentleness
When the poor tired child, Passion, falls asleep.
How far away the stars seem, and how far
Is our first kiss, and ah, how old my heart!"
Pensive they paced along the faded leaves,
While slowly he whose hand held hers replied:
"Passion has often worn our wandering hearts."

It is like a poem dictated in a dream, beautiful but half-real; his later poetry was to show up its inadequacy. The words sorrow and beauty recur again and again in this poetry, and generally associated with them such epithets as weary, wandering, dreaming, mournful. The beautiful first verse of "The Rose of the World" contains a small anthology of them:

> Who dreamed that beauty passes like a dream?
> For these red lips, with all their mournful pride,
> Mournful that no new wonder may betide,
> Troy passed away in one high funeral gleam,
> And Usna's children died.

These lines have more reality than the first passage, for Maud Gonne has come into them. Yeats had learned too by then from the French symbolists, introduced to his notice by Arthur Symons, another influence; and a new skill from the versification of the Rhymers' Club, that of Lionel Johnson above all; and a deepened sense of time from the Irish myths.

It may be that his passivity during these years was necessary to him; his poverty and shyness needed images of sadness and reassurance. At an early stage in his life this poem of William Morris was his favorite description of happiness:

> Midways of a walled garden,
>   In the happy poplar land,
>   Did an ancient castle stand,
> With an old knight for a warden.

Many scarlet bricks there were
  In its walls, and old grey stone;
  Over which red apples shone
At the right time of the year.

On the bricks the green moss grew,
  Yellow lichen on the stone,
  Over which red apples shone;
Little war that castle knew.

"Little war that castle knew": he needed a sense of sad remoteness from his own troubles, his indigence and inexperience; remoteness perhaps above all.

Yeats's passiveness during those first thirty years of his life has an appearance of weakness, but only an appearance. For, through it he drank in all the impressions that floated toward it, and most of them were retained all his life: the high idea of art, the esoteric knowledge, the old Irish stories, the admiration for aristocratic grace and peasant imagination never left him. Even when he was writing his greatest poetry he could resume the passive state which had served him so well. We know that Ezra Pound influenced him then, and in the Crazy Jane songs Louis MacNeice has traced the influence of Synge. While appearing to float unresistingly in the stream of those early years, before two women — Maud Gonne and Lady Gregory — forced him to become a man of action, he was appropriating the resources which he was to use after he gave himself his own voice.

He tells us that when he was a young man he was ill at ease with people. Yet he could not do without company, and drew life from what others were thinking and doing. He was affected immediately by their ideas. *The Wind Among the Reeds*, the last perfection of his early style, appeared in 1899, and John Eglinton complained that Yeats "looks too much away from himself and from his age, does not feel the facts of life enough, but seeks in art an escape from them." Still under the spell of the Rhymers' Club and the French symbolists, Yeats wrote:

I believe that the renewal of belief, which is the great movement of our time, will more and more liberate the arts from "their age" and from life, and leave them more and more free to lose themselves in beauty, and to busy themselves like all the great poetry of the past and like religions of all times, with "old faiths, myths and dreams," the accumulated beauty of the age.

Yet by five years later something else must have worked upon him, perhaps his own conscience, for, as he wrote to AE. then:

In my "Land of Heart's Desire" and in some of my lyric verse of that time there is an exaggeration of sentiment and sentimental beauty which I have come to think unmanly. . . . . I have been fighting the prevailing decadence for years, and have just got it underfoot in my own heart — it is sentiment and sentimental sadness, a womanish introspection . . . . As so often happens with a thing one has been tempted by and is still a little tempted by, I am roused by it to a kind of frenzied hatred which is quite out of my control.

There is a hint there of the rages in his later poems. And he writes in an essay:

We must ascend out of common interests, the thoughts of the newspapers, of the market-place, of men of science, but only so far as we can carry the normal, passionate, reasoning self, the personality as a whole.

The passionate, reasoning self, the personality as a whole, is what speaks in Yeats's later poetry. How did this come about? There is no facile explanation. His love for Maud Gonne, the troubles it brought him, and the repeated disappointments, must have turned him from his dreams and confronted him with life. They made him very unhappy. To escape from his frustration he had an affair with a woman in London whom Mr. Norman Jeffares calls Diana Vernon; it was not her real name. When Maud Gonne, on a short visit to London, asked to come and dine with him, he would not let her; yet after that the Vernon affair soon ended. There was another a few years later. Then in 1903 Yeats received a telegram informing him that Maud Gonne had married John MacBride, the Irish nationalist. She left her husband two years later, but Yeats still continued to see her, and, though saddened by the fantastic plots she had become involved in, still wanted to marry her. MacBride was killed in the Easter Rising of 1916, and Yeats went over to France and asked Maud again to marry him. When she refused he proposed to her adopted daughter Iseult, who also rejected him. He was then fifty-one, and had first met Maud about twenty-eight years before, when, as he says, "the trouble of my life began." How could these long years of alternating hope and disappointment fail to have had an effect upon him?

These were also the years when he learned to be a man of action. But he was a special man of action, or at least he professed it. In a letter written to Mrs. Shakespear, long after, he says: "It is curious how one's life falls into definite sections. — In 1897 a new scene was set, new actors appeared." It was characteristic of him that he saw the cockpit of Irish politics as a stage, and the figures as actors, and himself as one who had to play a part. About this time, or a little after, he became interested in the "mask," what he called the antithetical self. In an entry in his diary when he was forty-five he wrote: "I see always this one thing, that in practical life the Mask is more than the face." Some weeks later there is another entry:

I suppose that I may learn at last to keep to my own in every situation of life. To discover and create in myself as I grow old that thing which is to life what style is to letters — moral radiance, a personal quality of universal meaning in action and thought.

He became preoccupied with the problem of the whole man. He wrote in his diary:

I have before me an ideal expression in which all that I have, clay and spirit, assist; it is as though I most approximate towards that expression when I carry with me the greatest possible amount of hereditary thought and feeling, even national and family hatred and pride.

He had worn the mask of the poet, and worn it, or so it seemed, successfully. His wish now was to make him-

self a great figure, so that the figure might add greatness
to the man, and with such a basis the man might become
a great poet. He complained to H. W. Nevinson that
Byron was the last *man* who had written poetry: a re-
vealing choice. Even his study of magic may have helped
in the transformation; for magic not only tries to trans-
mute what it acts upon; it cannot but produce a greater
change in the magician. What we feel when we compare
Yeats's early style with his later, is that he is no longer
subject to his preoccupations — Irish myth, magical
knowledge, symbolism, hatred of abstraction — all he
had absorbed from his friends and his experience; that
he has now mastered them and can use them. He has
made himself into a public figure, and speaks to an au-
dience. He had achieved this by dramatizing himself,
and acting the role which was really himself. He knew
it, and once said to John Sparrow: "You must always re-
member your audience; it is always there and you can-
not write without it." Before this he had written for
many years for other poets, or for those who would have
liked to be poets. After his marriage in 1917, Mr. Jef-
fares says: "He had come to share experience common
to all men; domesticity and parenthood; he had also that
experience of the responsibility of power common to so
many great figures in English literature: Chaucer, Mil-
ton, Dryden, Swift." And in the poem, "Among School
Children" he could see himself half-ironically, yet ob-
jectively, as

A sixty-year-old smiling public man.

A public man is a man who is entitled to be listened to by the public; a great public man is one who can tell his public, on occasion, what he thinks of them, knowing that they will listen. This was the position which Yeats achieved, alone among the poets of his time. His public was first of all Irish, and it is easier to be the voice of a small nation than of a great one. His voice reached farther, of course, than Ireland, and was heard in many countries. But it was to the Irish that he spoke, as one who knew them, loved and hated them, admired and detested them. He was bound to them as much by his faults as his virtues; above all by his apparently inexhaustible reserves of Original Sin. Perhaps this is the most real and intimate relation a poet can have to a public in our time, as a great faulty image, in which they can find their own faults and their own hidden greatness; and Yeats was fortunate in drawing his audience from a country small, "backward," and still comparatively free from the spirit of abstraction which was spreading its blight over the greater nations. His struggle with Ireland helped to make him:

> I ranted to the knave and fool,
> But outgrew that school,
> Would transform the part,
> Fit audience found, but cannot rule
> My fanatic heart.
> . . . . . .
> Out of Ireland have we come.
> Great hatred, little room,
> Maimed us at the start.

W. B. YEATS

I carry from my mother's womb
A fanatic heart.

His contradictory feelings for Ireland are expressed in a letter he wrote to *The Observer* in 1917. Sir Hugh Lane had left his collection of French paintings to the National Gallery in London, disgusted by the scurrilous reception his offer of them to Dublin had roused there. Later he added a codicil to his will offering them to Dublin after all, but died before it was witnessed. Yeats says that, "in letters to Lady Gregory, who always pleaded for Ireland and the work there," Lane had spoken "of Ireland with great bitterness." He goes on:

I myself printed, as a pamphlet, "Poems written in Discouragement, 1912–1913" and certainly these poems are as bitter as the letters . . . That is the manner of our intemperate Irish nature (and I think that Elizabethan English were as volatile); we are quick to speak against our countrymen, but slow to give up our work. I once said to John Synge, "Do you write out of love or hate for Ireland?" and he replied, "I have often asked myself that question," and yet no success outside Ireland seemed of interest to him. Sir Hugh Lane wrote and felt bitterly, and yet when the feeling was at its height, while the Dublin slanders were sounding in his ears, he made a will leaving all he possessed, except the French pictures, to a Dublin gallery. A few days after writing that Ireland had so completely "disillusioned" him that he could not even bear "to hear of his early happy days in Galway," he bequeathed to Dublin an incomparable treasure.

Yeats was proud of being an Irishman, and still prouder of belonging to the Anglo-Irish ascendency,

53

which had contributed so many names to Irish history and literature. He could therefore write more bitterly of Ireland than any of its enemies, because more intimately. He became a public man and a public poet because he shared that love and that fury and had a voice to give them utterance.

It was in his poetry he found that voice. His prose to the end has a curious indecision, and is filled with ideas put as rhetorical questions, a great trick of his. The word "perhaps" recurs persistently, even when he is setting down a thought which, one would have imagined, must have been of the utmost importance to him. In prose he seems to have felt that his mind was at liberty to wander, and his ideas as well. His prose is exact when he describes George Moore, whom he detested, or when he writes of Bernard Shaw, whom he respected and disliked. He can be witty then in quite a different style from his poetry:

Shaw was right to claim Samuel Butler for his master, for Butler was the first Englishman to make the discovery that it is possible to write with great effect without music, without style, either good or bad. . . . Presently I had a nightmare that I was haunted by a sewing-machine, that clicked and shone, but the incredible thing was that the machine smiled, smiled perpetually.

Yeats's "Autobiographies" are delightful for such touches as this. But compare this kind of satire even with a poem written when he was still finding his second voice:

"Better go down upon your marrow-bones
And scrub a kitchen pavement, or break stones
Like an old pauper, in all kinds of weather;
For to articulate sweet sounds together
Is to work harder than all these, and yet
Be thought an idler by the noisy set
Of bankers, schoolmasters, and clergymen
The martyrs call the world."

He was uncertain among ideas, even those he clung to all his life. He had to embody them imaginatively before he was convinced by them. Even that curious compilation, *A Vision*, which was dictated to him, he says, by communicators speaking through the voice of his wife in a series of trances, and which gave him a complete chart of the cycles of time and all the phases within them; even from that he disengaged himself, with the excuse that the communicators were sent to him to provide his poetry with imagery.

I have been concerned with the poet and his audience, and the disappearance of the audience. Yeats, it seems to me, had a genuine audience, not a scattered sprinkling of readers in Dublin, London, New York, Paris, and the universities. He gathered together an audience to which he could address himself, and which gave him the liberty to speak of anything, while obliging him to speak of certain things. He was bound to speak of Ireland, its politics, its heroisms, its feuds, and the glories of its past; to speak of them in sorrow and anger:

Romantic Ireland's dead and gone,
It's with O'Leary in the grave,

or in grief and wonder, of those who died in the Easter Rising:

> I write it out in a verse —
> MacDonagh and MacBride
> And Connolly and Pearse
> Now and in time to be,
> Wherever green is worn,
> Are changed, changed utterly:
> A terrible beauty is born.

He was also free to speak of anything else he chose: Troy, Byzantium, the Great Memory, the moon, youth and age, the talk of his fellow writers, the nature of poetry, time and immortality, the gossip of Dublin, the disreputable loves of Crazy Jane, and above all himself, and the dialogue between himself and his soul. No other poet of his time had such a variety of theme and mood, ranging from the exalted to the Rabelaisian. He was free even to be obscure, but obscure through some fine excess, as in the two great poems on Byzantium. It might be said that he could afford to be obscure, because he had an audience. He had mastered his art so completely that he could express all his moods with equal power. There is the high contemplative reverie, as in "Prayer for My Daughter":

> An intellectual hatred is the worst,
> So let her think opinions are accurst.
> Have I not seen the loveliest woman born
> Out of the mouth of Plenty's horn,
> Because of her opinionated mind
> Barter that horn and every good

By quiet natures understood
For an old bellows full of angry wind?

And may her bridegroom bring her to a house
Where all's accustomed, ceremonious;
For arrogance and hatred are the wares
Peddled in the thoroughfares.
How but in custom and in ceremony
Are innocence and beauty born?
Ceremony's a name for the rich horn,
And custom for the spreading laurel tree.

He is praying that his daughter should not be like Maud
Gonne, and yet, in spite of that one violent line refer-
ring to the bellows full of angry wind, the poem has a
high dignity. Then, "A Dialogue of Self and Soul" is
a rhetorical confession of a secret conflict; and rhetoric
is a public art.

I am content to follow to its source
Every event in action or in thought;
Measure the lot; forgive myself the lot!
When such as I cast out remorse
So great a sweetness flows into the breast,
We must laugh and we must sing,
We are blest by everything,
Everything we look upon is blest.

And there are the single lines or short passages in the
grand style, which draw their power from that rhetorical
intoxication of a man conscious of being listened to:

I knew a phoenix in my youth, so let them have their day

and

Homer is my example and his unchristened heart . . .

and

> I am accustomed to their lack of breath,
> But not that my dear friend's dear son,
> Our Sidney and our perfect man,
> Could share in that discourtesy of death.

But perhaps his most consummate triumphs are in his simple riddling songs, filled with the realistic yet credulous imagination of the peasantry:

> As I came over Windy Gap
> They threw a halfpenny into my cap,
> For I am running to Paradise;
> And all that I need do is to wish
> And somebody puts his hand in the dish
> To throw me a bit of salted fish:
> *And there the king is but as the beggar.*
> . . . . . .
>
> Poor men have grown to be rich men,
> And rich men grown to be poor again,
> And I am running to Paradise;
> And many a darling wit's grown dull
> That tossed a bare heel when at school,
> Now it has filled an old sock full:
> *And there the king is but as the beggar.*

That is the kind of song the peasantry might make if they still made songs, with its shrewd satirical evaluation of worldly good, and its belief in another world. The songs of Crazy Jane are written out of the peasant judgment of the world, and at their best rise to a heroic vision of life:

Banners choke the sky;
Men-at-arms tread;
Armoured horses neigh
Where the great battle was
In the narrow pass:
All things remain in God.

The peasant believes more strongly than any other class
in another world, and is attached more closely by his
vocation to this one. The same image of the world is
repeated in the song of Tom the Lunatic:

Whatever stands in field or flood,
Bird, beast, fish or man,
Mare or stallion, cock or hen,
Stands in God's unchanging eye
In all the vigour of its blood;
In that faith I live or die.

In these songs it was the unwritten judgment of the
peasantry that found utterance in that very extraordi-
nary public man. Yet he could follow with a poem in
which he sees:

Scattered on the level grass
Or winding through the grove
Plato there and Minos pass,
There stately Pythagoras
And all the choir of Love.

He had his own privileges.

I have tried to trace how a poet became a man, and
the man in his turn became a poet, with all his qualities,
good and bad, his experience, passion, wisdom, faults,

prejudices, rages, fancies — and how with all these behind or within him he could gain the confidence to address men and women. A poet who regards poetry as a métier which must not be disturbed by anything outside it is not fully human, but a sort of specialist; with the most honorable intentions he cuts himself off from the life which would fructify his art. Robert Graves says that a poet writes only for other poets; and certainly he himself has written some of the most beautiful poetry of his time. But Yeats took the other road, and his powers immensely expanded, and his style put on authority.

He confessed his faith in a letter to Lady Dorothy Wellesley. After blaming himself for having been unfair to the poetry of Laura Riding, and her intricate intensity, he went on:

This difficult work, which is being written everywhere now (a professor from Barcelona tells me they have it there) has the substance of philosophy & is a delight to the poet with his professional pattern; but it is not your road or mine, & ours is the main road, the road of naturalness & swiftness and we have thirty centuries upon our side. We alone can "think like a wise man, yet express ourselves like the common people." These new men are goldsmiths working with a glass screwed into one eye, whereas we stride ahead of the crowd . . . looking to right & left. "To right and left" by which I mean that we need like Milton, Shakespere, Shelley, vast sentiments, generalizations supported by tradition.

But also the touch of nature which makes the whole world kin.

✽   ✽   ✽

CRITICISM AND THE POET

O ne of the functions of criticism is to open out the riches of literature for us and help us to enjoy them. This is probably its most useful function — to be a helpful intermediary between literature and the reader — and it has a duty to both. Goethe tells us that his eyes were opened to a new world by Lessing; writers still remain indebted to Coleridge, and more recently to T. S. Eliot. A hundred years ago Matthew Arnold insisted on the importance for the poet of a free circulation of fresh and true ideas adapted to his age, and this he regarded as the task of criticism to provide. These are two of the chief functions which criticism can fulfill, and in the greatest critics they are indistinguishable. In our time the best criticism has been more and more confined to a different task, that of analysis and interpretation, and the work of intermediation has been left to critics of less contemporary repute. I cannot help feeling that the gap between poetry and its potential audience is due partly to this cause.

The value of criticism as an intermediary is obvious. The great virtue of criticism of this kind lies in its capacity for admiration, that indispensable virtue. If we turn to the romantic critics — Lamb, Hazlitt, and Coleridge — that is what we find, and we recognize it as springing from a largeness of soul, a capacity to delight in all that is great. A good critic in this style is one who apprehends by a native affinity the virtues of a work of imagination and rejoices in them. Corresponding to him is the bad critic who sees faults more clearly than virtues, and sometimes fails to see what is done because he sees so clearly the points at which it is done badly. By his powers of admiration Ruskin remains a great critic of art; by his lack of the same powers Carlyle is one of the worst of critics. In the nineteenth century criticism was divided between the schools of admiration and fault-finding, but at its best it followed in the track of Lamb and Hazlitt; Swinburne was in the succession, and so was Arnold himself, with qualifications insisted upon by himself. In the universities toward the end of the century there were figures like Saintsbury, Quiller-Couch, Raleigh, and Sir Herbert Grierson, who transmitted their love of poetry to their students in lectures and to the general public in books. They did this by a sort of natural compulsion. Their admiration for poetry was so great that they could not keep it to themselves, but had to share it with as many others as they could find. They were men of learning and long experience, and among them were great scholars like Sir Herbert Grierson. The influence they had was wide and beneficent; they wakened in young and older readers an interest in poetry and imaginative literature which might otherwise have remained dormant. Their kind of criticism, animated by admiration but not without judgment, is very rare today.

The other kind, represented sometimes by Arnold on his self-conscious side but denied by his practice, is the representative criticism of our time. It is not concerned with the propagation of a wide interest in poetry; it does not seek for converts among the public. It is addressed mainly to those who have to study poetry in any case, to university students and secondary school boys; and apart from these to the readers who may be assumed to know poetry already, but can be put in the way of knowing it more precisely by analyzing their feelings while they read some poem, or analyzing some poem while their feelings stand watching. This kind of criticism has made people read poems more carefully, and that no doubt is to the good. When the critic is himself a poet, like John Crowe Ransom or William Empson, or when he has an unusual imaginative grasp of poetry and language, like I. A. Richards, he can discover in poetry new meanings and new sources of delight for us. He can extract or distill from a poem meanings which a more ordinary acquaintance with it would pass by without notice. And Mr. Richards has shown that criticism can also make us aware of our stock responses, which sometimes conceal what the poem is actually saying.

The main point of this new criticism is to establish what the poem really means, linguistically. Yet there is another way of coming to know a poem, a way which does not hold up its movement (and that is of great importance) even at passages which are not immediately understood, but runs as it reads, keeping pace with the rhythmical pulse. To examine a poem curiously, arresting it every now and then to scrutinize a line, a phrase, or a word, and slowing down its movement, may bring fresh knowledge, and the knowledge may generate a new emotion, but the new emotion may not be the emotion of the poem itself. Too thoroughly applied, this method may sometimes elicit from the poem a set of meanings quite different from those which strike the reader when he first comes to it. Some of those meanings may really throw light on the poem, and the reader may return to it and read it again as if for the first time, and yet read it differently. But if this does not happen, if the poem, having been submitted to analysis, does not assume a new yet natural shape, what remains is merely the analysis with its own internal interest; and the poem has been replaced by the criticism.

I had better at this point bring an example, and I shall take it from one of the most brilliant of contemporary writers on poetry, almost equally delightful and exasperating: William Empson. At the beginning of *Seven Types of Ambiguity*, he says: "The fundamental situation, whether it deserves to be called ambiguous or not, is that a word or a grammatical structure is effective in several ways at once." That is true; and Mr. Empson has made us aware of it in a new way. He goes on:

To take a famous example, there is no pun, double syntax, or dubiety of feeling, in

Bare ruined choirs, where late the sweet birds sang,

but the comparison holds for many reasons; because ruined monastery choirs are places in which to sing, because they involve sitting in a row, because they are made of wood, are carved into knots and so forth, because they used to be surrounded by a sheltering building crystallised out of the likeness of a forest, and coloured with stained glass and painting like flowers and leaves, because they are now abandoned by all but the grey walls coloured like the skies of winter, because the cold and Narcissistic charm suggested by choir-boys suits well with Shakespeare's feeling for the object of the Sonnets, and for various sociological and historical reasons (the protestant destruction of monasteries; fear of puritanism), which it would be hard now to trace out in their proportions; these reasons, and many more relating the simile to its place in the Sonnet, must all combine to give the line its beauty, and there is a sort of ambiguity in not knowing which of them to hold most clearly in mind. Clearly this is involved in all such richness and heightening of effect, and the machinations of ambiguity are among the very roots of poetry.

Shakespeare's line has certainly a rich and heightened effect, and the effect comes partly from the ambiguity of poetic language. Mr. Empson is concerned here rather with the vast and intricate world he has charted so well, than with criticism. The line itself is merely an object, starting from which he sets out to discover how ambiguity brings about its effects. By exercise of imagination he creates a world of his own, enjoyable in itself, but not enjoyable in the way that the line of poetry is enjoyable. After this journey we return to the line, and wonder how on earth it ever managed by such labyrinthine wanderings to get where it is. What Mr. Empson does with it is not, and is not intended to be except very remotely, connected with criticism. Regarded as criticism, the real objection to it is not that it tells us something about a line in a sonnet, but that it tells us far too much, and provides us with such an abundance of associations that the clear and immediate meaning is buried under them. Mr. Empson is trying to guess at the things which might have been in Shakespeare's mind, or in language itself, without Shakespeare's knowing it. Among these may have been the dissolution of the monasteries; the forest-like appearance of a Gothic chapel; even the fact that choir-boys sit in rows, even the fact, though I doubt it, that Shakespeare was thinking of choir-boys when he wrote of sweet birds. We can keep these possibilities in mind if we are contemplating the vast and strange world of poetic ambiguity; but, if we think of them and the line of poetry together, they break it into a chaotic confusion of absurd pictures. The position now is that the method, which Mr. Empson used so fruitfully for inquiring into poetic ambiguity, seems actually to have been taken over since by criticism, with slight modification.

This method consists in reading into a poem all sorts of probable or possible meanings apart from the clear and obvious one, and there is an example of it in Mr. Cleanth Brooks's critical volume, *The Well Wrought Urn*. There he has an essay entitled "The Motivation of Tennyson's Weeper," the subject of which is "Tears, Idle Tears." The poem is not particularly obscure, yet this is how Mr. Brooks deals with it:

> Any account of the poem may very well begin with a consideration of the nature of the tears. Are they *idle* tears? Or are they not rather the most meaningful of tears? Does not the very fact that they are "idle" (that is, tears occasioned by no immediate grief) become in itself a guarantee of the fact that they spring from a deeper, more universal cause?

Then he notes that the tears " 'rise in the heart' — for all that they have been first announced as 'idle.' " From this there is only a step to "the question of whether Tennyson is guilty of (or to be complimented upon) a use of paradox may well wait upon further discussion."

But here another problem confronts us, for the tears also rise

> In looking at the happy autumn fields
> And thinking of the days that are no more.

Mr. Brooks continues: "The poet himself does not stand responsible for any closer linkage between these actions" — I take it he means by the actions the tears rising in Tennyson's eyes, his looking at the happy autumn fields, and his thinking of the days that are no more — "though, as a matter of fact, most of us will want to make a closer linkage here." He goes on: "For, if we change 'happy Autumn-fields,' say, to 'happy April-fields,' the two terms tend to draw apart." I think that by the two terms Mr. Brooks must mean the looking and the weeping, or he may mean simply that April is far from autumn. The poem by now has receded into a remote academic distance, where we can hardly recognize, far less feel it.

Mr. Brooks is a critic of more than ordinary intelligence, and what he says about the general character of poetry in *The Well Wrought Urn* is sometimes illuminating. But when he deals with a specific poem he often seems to me to mistake it for another poem that has never been written. This is due to two reasons: the undeviating scrutiny which he turns on the poem, to me a mistaken kind of scrutiny; and his theory of poetry which implies that it should always include, as necessary elements, paradox and irony. To know or to think one knows the qualities which must always distinguish poetry is dangerous, for then we shall find them in it whether they are there or not. In searching for the meaning which he had persuaded himself must be in "Tears, Idle Tears," Mr. Brooks had to ignore the obvious meaning. There is no real contradiction, after all, between the idleness of the tears and their rising in the heart, for the movements of the heart, too, may be idle. Yet in speaking of "idle tears" I think it is obvious that Tennyson meant nothing more than that they were of no effect, and changed nothing. I shall not follow Mr. Brooks any further in his analysis of the poem, but I confess that this kind of criticism, so thorough and so mistaken, seems to me of very little use to any reader, and that for myself it gives me a faint touch of claustrophobia, the feeling that I am being confined in a narrow place with the poem and the critic, and that I shall not get away until all three of us are exhausted. The great danger of this kind of criticism is that it shuts the poem in upon itself as an object, not of enjoyment but of scrutiny, and cuts it off from the air which it should breathe and its spontaneous operation on those who are capable of receiving it. Everything is slowed down or arrested; the poem cannot get on; the movement, and the movement of a poem is an essential part of it, is held up, while we examine its parts in isolation. One thinks of a laboratory; and indeed the analysis of poetry, pushed to this length, resembles a scientific test.

What is the natural response to poetry and what is the nature of its operation on us? I have mentioned the dialogue of Plato in which Socrates cross-examined Ion, the rhapsodist. Ion confessed that at the most affecting scenes of the *Iliad* he was deeply and visibly moved, and that his audience wept, with eyes fixed earnestly on him, and overcome by his declamation. The behavior of the audience becomes more understandable if we accept Mr. Richards' classification of the meanings which we may find in poetry; the meaning expressed in sense, in feeling, in tone, and in intention; and remember the importance which he assigns to feeling. All of us can learn a great deal from what Mr. Richards says about these things, and I want to consider now what our feelings are when we first discover poetry, for these should give us an idea how they can be fostered and developed.

I shall take the illustration of a young man in love. When we are young it is natural for us, given the disposition, to fall in love with poetry. Sometimes we desert it later; sometimes with good fortune the attachment is life-long. All of us who have felt it can remember that encounter, which seemed to open out the feelings and the imagination, as love does, and made us happy and vulnerable in a world not eminently sympathetic to poetry. This is the state in which our dealings with poetry begin; if we miss it we miss almost everything; and if we encounter poetry in some other way, early or late, we are likely to see it as a dry study or as an intellectual discipline. This first discovery of poetry requires from teachers and critics the most sensitive consideration and the most scrupulous respect.

Take a young man who has fallen in love for the first time, and imagine him having love exhaustively explained to him by someone who knows a great deal about it, perhaps too much, by experience. If the young man is very simple, as he is likely to be, think of his consulting next some psychologist willing to explain to him what love really is in its psychological aspect. At last, in despair, imagine him turning to Bernard Shaw and learning from him that love is merely a device of the Life Force, which flings men and women into each other's arms without regard to them or their wishes or their happiness. The young man will receive a shock, and, if he has a heart and mind of his own, will probably repent of his inquiries and feel some shame at having asked people who are not in love to answer his questions about love; and he will go away with the conviction that this is not love as he knows it. There are ways of knowing love, and ways of knowing about it; ways of knowing poetry and knowing about it. Marcel Proust exemplifies the dangers of loving and knowing too much, of experiencing love and simultaneously analyzing it. Sometimes in his great novels the analysis of love begins almost with the emotion; doubt is there from the start, and the lover learns what he does not want to learn and perhaps does not need to learn. What love says, and what love means, and the deep divergence between appearance and reality, become insoluble problems.

I do not want to carry this comparison to absurd lengths. I wish merely to recall how vulnerable and impressionable we were when we first discovered poetry, and how easily our feelings might have been diverted from their natural course even by too much knowledge, or too much instruction given too early. (The instruction begins unluckily in the schools, as it is.) Plato recommended a discipline for those who wanted to understand objects of beauty. The student was advised to contemplate beautiful objects in an ascending scale of excellence, until he became worthy at last to perceive what beauty is in itself. There is a natural progression in the

understanding of poetry, and the discipline for acquir-
ing it is much the same as Plato's. We learn about poetry
from poetry, and we can go on learning until we have
no longer much interest in asking what poetry is. Analy-
sis, especially if it is applied too early, makes the poem
into a problem instead of an experience. And if the be-
ginner is unlucky, it may become a problem before it
has ever been an experience. He will set about analyzing
it without having heard "the true voice of feeling," and
discover a great number of things about it without hav-
ing been moved by it. I have chosen an extreme but not
an improbable example so that I might outline a real
distinction. To the young particularly, even the wisest
supervision, if it comes before it should, may do harm.
If the young can find no Platonic guide to lead them
through the whole range of poetry to the greatest poetry
of all, it seems better for them to plunge into poetry by
themselves, and to read as much of it and of every kind
of it as they can, with full understanding, half-under-
standing, even misunderstanding, accepting the dangers
of the enterprise, than to be strictly schooled. They will
learn in the best way, by enjoyment and disappointment,
and what they learn will be their own. When they want
to know, as they naturally will, what others think of the
poetry they have read, they will turn to the critics for
guidance and illumination. In time they will be ready to
see that there are criteria of poetry. That seems to me the
natural induction into poetry and the natural progres-
sion through it. How schools and universities can accom-

modate themselves to this I cannot say, or how critics are to encourage and foster it. Yet, to set up standards at the start, to advise the young enthusiast what he should find in poetry before he has any knowledge of it, is an unnatural proceeding; and if a strict method of reading poetry is superadded, the situation becomes worse. One may argue that this will save the young reader from making mistakes which he otherwise might have made; but there is the greater danger that it may instill in him an attitude quite at variance with the feelings which a poem evokes. And, if the teacher is devoid of sensibility, as is sometimes bound to happen, the method becomes a sort of machine through which the poem is put so as to achieve a result already in the teacher's mind. The situation is made more dangerous by the fact that analysis itself can become a fascinating occupation; I have met students who say that they find it endlessly interesting.

The demand for strictness in criticism comes from other quarters than the practicians of this kind of criticism. Harold Osborne in a book on *Aesthetics and Criticism* some time ago made the following demand on criticism:

To be useful to aesthetics — or to itself — criticism must be coherent. In so far as criticism involves assessments of comparative worth or excellence, it is obvious that unless the critics all agree to mean the same thing, and the right thing, when they formulate judgements about the goodness or badness of works of art, their pronouncements must remain a pudder of anomalous and desultory ejaculations which have no value for aesthetics until the standards of excellence as-

sumed by each individual critic have been coordinated into
a systematic unity.

To ask for this is to ask for the moon, or for a perfect
impersonal machine. Mr. Osborne's aesthetics are impos-
ing and throw light on the general laws of art. But, in
demanding conformity from the critics he is acting in
much the same way as a professor of moral philosophy
might act if he demanded that his theory of ethics should
rule us in making our practical decisions. Mr. Osborne
forgets that critics have to deal with poems not poetry,
novels not fiction, paintings not painting; and deal with
them in their uniqueness, using as they best can their
particular sensibility, and their unavoidable tastes, which
are also unique. Whatever the rules he may have accepted
on theoretical grounds, or discovered for himself, the
critic is left finally to discern by his own sensibility the
excellences and the faults of the unique work he is con-
sidering, whether it is "King Lear," *Paradise Lost, Tris-
tram Shandy*, the "Ode on a Grecian Urn," *Pride and
Prejudice*, "The Waste Land," or the whole rowdy mob
of the world's masterpieces. I do not think that Mr. Os-
borne's theories will help him there very much; he will
depend rather on a long experience of all kinds of writ-
ing, by which he has learned to distinguish their quali-
ties and assess them, just as in the course of living we
imperfectly learn to distinguish and assess the qualities
of people we meet. And fortified by that experience he
may say something about a writer he intimately under-
stands which no one else could have said.

There is no infallible guide to the practice of criticism. Mr. Osborne's demands, if they were complied with, would put the critic in chains; and the new critic, sticking scrupulously to his formula, can be much worse than the old. Mr. Brooks's words on Tennyson's poem persistently recur to me, as if they were a warning: "Any account of the poem may very well begin with a consideration of the nature of the tears." That seems a very strange, a more than legal, way of seizing upon a poem; and almost as strange is that Mr. Brooks should try to establish, word by word, like a scout following a difficult trail, that Tennyson was expressing a paradox, when the whole poem is clearly the expression of a paradox. I accept the word as Mr. Brooks uses it, though I would not choose it myself: the intensity of feeling in the poem makes it inadequate and inappropriate. Tennyson is speaking over and over again in the poem of the death in life of memory, saying in image after image that memory brings our dead friends up from the underworld and sinks with them beneath the verge, and that it is as sad as remembered kisses after death. If we follow the poem as closely as Mr. Brooks does, and in his mood which is so unlike its mood, we lose its feeling and are left with an object stranded on some shore where it could never have been expected to find itself. The new criticism was salutary enough while it remained an influence; it was a useful counterirritant against all sorts of loose and sentimental criticism. But from an influence it has become a sanctioned method, and a method, once it is established, becomes in spite of itself an instrument of power. It determines standards, and dictates to the critic and to the poet. I should say that there are poets who must be daunted by the reflection that, if they venture upon a poem, they may find it being put through that formidable mill.

Among the public this kind of criticism cannot but give the impression that a poem is something to be analyzed and not to be enjoyed. Against this idea I am thankful to have the support of a great poet and a great critic. Some time ago T. S. Eliot gave a talk to the Authors' Club in London. For what he said I have to rely on a newspaper report. The report quotes him as saying:

Several influences converge nowadays towards the belief that to appreciate and enjoy poetry is to explain it, and that the way to explain it is to explain it away. To understand a poem it is first of all necessary to be moved by it, and to be aware of the way in which one is moved. . . . A genuine poem may arouse a great number of differing individual responses, yet there will be always something in common between them. That is what a poem is for. . . . Nowadays school children are made to study not only a few standard texts, as of Shakespeare and Milton, but even the work of living poets, so that they have less and less opportunity to discover poetry for themselves without having it explained to them.

These are obviously only a few sentences chosen by the reporter from Mr. Eliot's speech. He also reported Mr. Eliot as saying at the beginning that "criticism of poetry began and ended in enjoyment," which I think is the traditional practice. But the observation that is most illuminating in this report is that "a genuine poem may arouse a very great number of differing responses, yet there will be always something in common between them," and that this is what poetry is for. There have been some very strange responses to poems, as Mr. Richards has shown so convincingly in his book, *Practical Criticism*, responses which seemed plainly to contradict one another. Yet, even allowing for this, there will be something in common between people's varied responses to a poem, and the poem exists for that purpose. If we believe this, poetry takes on a wider significance than it is currently allowed, and lets in the ordinary unanalytical reader, and with him human nature. People will read poetry for enjoyment, since that is what it is intended for; and they will not, except in a few exceptional cases, take it up as a strict methodical study. And it may be said that they will get more help, both in enjoyment and understanding, from the traditional critic who tells them what the poem means to him, than from the new one who warns them that it cannot possibly mean what it appears to mean, so that he has no choice left but to explain it. The divorce between the public audience and the poet is widened by this critical method; or perhaps one should rather say that the method legalizes the divorce as a settled and normal state. And that is what we feel to be wrong.

* * *

POETRY AND THE POET

I want to say a few things about poetry, the forms in which it is embodied and the spirit which animates these forms. The forms range from the simple folk song and ballad to the poetic comedy and tragedy and the epic. Regarding poetry in its extent, we find there an extraordinary variety of forms and discover that they all have a purpose and a wonderful suitability. Looking back over the history of poetry, we see that endless invention and modification have gone into these forms, from the small compact sonnet to blank verse, the greatest inno-vation in English poetry. All these forms have an organic function, which is lacking in free verse. In our own time free verse has had a very considerable influence, which now seems to be passing. The main defect of free verse is monotony; it can be used apparently for any subject and any mood; there is no escape for the writer of free verse except into free verse. The whole world of forms, the whole variety of poetic expression, lies outside. The poet, it seems to me, attains his freedom through some given form or set of forms. There may well be new forms still to come, for language changes and may bring about the use of other rhythmical measures.

These metrical forms are subject to the accidents of time; they fall into disuse in ages when they are found to be unsuitable for the expression of contemporary feeling, and may later be revived when they become employable again. Through them poetry speaks to us not only in the speech of our time and out of the world we know, but from past ages, since they have existed for a long time, and connect the present with the past. The problem of communication is often discussed by poets and critics. In writing a poem should the poet have the conscious intention of communicating with his readers? This is a difficult question. Perhaps the intention to communicate is always there, though the poet may not be conscious of it. Yet, if he is to communicate something of value, his attention must obviously remain fixed on the poem. For it is the poem that communicates with us; and it does this, in great poetry, long after the poet's death. Perhaps this is because poetry is itself the communication of something for which no other kind of speech can serve; it is certainly not because the poet sets out with the idea that he must communicate. The discussions of contemporary poetry are beset with false problems. The more perfectly achieved a poem is, the more fully it will be apprehended by those who read it. Deliberate intention, anything which distracts the poet from what he seeks to express, may become an obstacle to understanding. A folk song that sings for its own pleasure will give back to us for centuries the emotion out of which it was born. And a story which is thinking of nothing but the story will move us most when we forget or do not know who is telling it.

The poetic story and the song move us partly because they are rhythmical and musical; but the rhythm and music would be extraneous and meaningless if they were not animated by imagination. By imagination I mean nothing so metaphysically hard to understand as Coleridge's definition of it, but rather a faculty which belongs to us all, in however fragmentary a degree. If we did not possess imagination in this sense, we would not be able to understand our neighbors and our friends even as imperfectly as we do, and life would be a blank for us: we would have no image of it. We would not be able even to gossip about our neighbors. Indeed, gossip is for many people the main form that imagination takes; for it involves invention and with that some rudimentary conception of life; at its common level it is a perpetual reminder that common men are subject to the same pleasures and griefs and the same absurd chances as the great. To make us feel the grief of Priam and Hecuba over the death of Hector, dead thirty centuries ago, is another thing, and far beyond the reach of gossip, yet it is not altogether different in kind. It is a high feat of imagination, and we could not respond to it if we were quite devoid of imagination ourselves.

By imagination I mean that power by which we apprehend living beings and living creatures in their individuality, as they live and move, and not as ideas or categories. The knowledge which it gives of Priam and Hecuba is of a different kind from that which history and archaeology can provide. It takes us into the feelings and thoughts of these legendary figures, and makes us feel the full weight and the uniqueness of their lives. It is as important as anything can be that we should be able to do this, for it makes us understand human life vividly and intimately in ourselves because we have felt it in others. Imagination gives us this knowledge of people and Nature, but never exact knowledge, since it cannot and does not wish to study them under the fixed conditions which make possible the exact knowledge of the scientist. The life and movement and individuality of human beings, and of beasts and birds and trees, their feelings and moods and mischances, are everything to it. Compared with science its scope is vague and incommensurable, since it embraces all possibilities of experience. Consequently, it is for human living that imagination is indispensable. Exact knowledge is only a fragment of the knowledge we need in order to live. We can have no exact knowledge of ourselves, far less of other people. There is no exact answer to the problems we are perpetually troubled by and have never solved; yet we must have some faculty by which we can deal with them. We cannot ask science to tell us whether our lives have a meaning, or why we should pursue good and avoid evil, or how we should live with our neighbors. Imagination does not answer these questions; perhaps the only answer for them is in faith. What imagination does is to give us a vivid sense of them. Such questions obstinately haunt us, and our lives would become barbarous if they ceased; we should not know or be ourselves in any human sense; we should become semi-abstractions, categories, somewhat like the figures described in George Orwell's book *1984.*

I have used the word imagination in a way which may seem to restrict it to poetry and imaginative literature, and to deny it to the scientist. That of course would be ridiculous. Perhaps the greatest intensity of imagination during the last hundred years, as well as the most intense intellectual passion, has gone into pure science. But the subjects which excite the imagination of the scientist, no matter in what branch of study, are different from those that move the imagination of the poet, and if I were to use the word in this extended sense I could not apply it with much relevance to the kind of knowledge, inexact yet essential for us, which is had by seeing into the life of things. That kind of imagination obviously had a greater sway in the earlier stages of civilization than it has now. Even less than four hundred years ago, in the Elizabethan age, poets exercised it more freely than we apparently can at present. Poetry, one might say, came more easily then to the writer than prose, and comedy and tragedy fell naturally into poetry, while, now that prose has become a broad river and poetry has dwindled into a narrow trickle, we have to use the most elaborate expedients to bring the poetic play back again. In Elizabeth's time prose itself was more suited for imagination than for thought. The great change, as we know, began in the seventeenth century and was carried to triumph in the age of reason; prose became the instrument of clear thought, and poetry for a time was forced to emulate it, so strong was the general tendency and the genuine need. Feeling and imagination were reinstated by the romantic poets, but the romantic impulse died in less than a hundred years; poetry faded into an echo in William Morris, and prose became the supreme form, universally acknowledged.

A process such as this, so imperious that it has changed the language in which we feel and think, must have had an influence, in countless ways, on our feelings and thoughts and our conception of human life. Its influence on poetry, though important enough, may be of less concern than its influence on these other things. Poetry has no quarrel with pure science, with the disinterested inquiry into the nature of things; for poetry is concerned in a different way with the same inquiry. But, if you have two great powers, both of them serviceable to human life, and one of them develops at a great speed while the other marks time, the result is bound to be dangerous. I can make only a speculative guess here. During the past three centuries, slowly at first, then more and more rapidly, the balance between the poetic imagination and the scientific intellect has been lost. Let us assume that this process began when people realized that by carefully observing and studying nature they might win mastery over it. Philosophers and scientists began to look forward to the acquisition of power over nature, yet what they had in mind was not pure but applied science, capable of creating a world such as ours but not to make us free. The thought that nature could be mastered evoked a great hope for the future of mankind, and when a hope is thrown open our energies irresistibly rush toward it. At the beginning this hope was cherished by philosophers only; but in due course it became the general hope of the Western world. A romanticism of science arose in the eighteenth century, and became almost universal in the nineteenth, the age of progress. People believed that science would work a vast transmutation on society, and bring in a sort of millennium. To measure the strength of that faith, one has only to read Macaulay's prophecy of the coming future, when universal prosperity and freedom would be the rule, and flourishing fields would cover the sides of Ben Nevis. Scientists as recent as Pasteur and Pavlov have believed in it. Few of us, whether scientists or laymen, believe in it now. We have learned that what the nineteenth century called progress has brought us where we are, and that, whenever the idea of progress is canvassed, something is left out of account. The dream of science has been justified in many ways. It has brought countless improvements in our daily life; without the dream our life would be much poorer. If the world created by science seems to us sometimes to have advanced too quickly and too far, while we have remained marking time on the same spot, that can be borne for the sake of the good that may come of it. If we feel sometimes that we are living in a future which does not fit us, that too can be borne. What imposes a greater strain on us, the real strain of modern life, is the sense, not of too much happening too quickly, but of something lacking. Something in the apparent progression has not progressed; for myself I would call it the imagination which would have made us able to use for purely human purposes all that applied science offers us. A lopsided development, whether of the body or the mind, is a diseased development, and is bound to lead to strange and unpredictable results. One of these is that people in general are troubled now by the thought of applied science, in spite of the benefits it has brought, increasing our wealth, lengthening our lives, and alleviating pain. The catalogue is endless. What we are troubled by is the sense that science has run on far ahead of us, and that we are without the wisdom to use for our good the enormous power which it drops in passing into our hands. As we do not know how to use that power, it becomes an ambiguous gift, an explosive possibility. This is the focus of the apprehension that fills the living world, and the subject that generally comes up when people gather together.

What do people mean, loosely, when they say that

science has become a danger? They obviously mean ap-
plied science and the power over things and human
beings which is made possible by it. They are daunted by
the world that applied science and centralized organiza-
tion have built around them; they are alarmed by the
thought of a future in which these powers will become
irresistible and inescapable. From this arise those occa-
sional nightmares which seem to warn us that the
ordinary human being may not be able to survive, to-
gether with the traditional beliefs and customs and feel-
ings which have fostered him and made him what he is.
You will find this nightmare described in the forlorn
Utopias of Aldous Huxley and George Orwell, which
prophesy the end of mankind and its supersession by a
species indistinguishable from it in outward appearance,
but without love, goodness, and evil, or even hatred, as
we have come to know them during our lives and the
history of civilization. Our imaginations, when they have
nothing better to do, project these vast, distorted night-
mares into the future. I think we all make these pro-
jections, for in states of apprehension or foreboding we
live more in the future than in the present, and are
troubled by both.

What can the imagination do with this world? Some-
thing different, surely, from the manufacture of the
nightmare. Hugo von Hofmannsthal said once that true
imagination is always conservative. By this he may have
meant that it keeps intact the bond which unites us with
the past of mankind, so that we can still understand

Odysseus and Penelope, and the people of the Old Testament. Or he may have meant something more: that imagination is able to do this because it sees the life of everyone as the endless repetition of a single pattern. It is hard to explain how we can enter into past lives if this is not so. We become human by repetition; in the imagination that repetition becomes an object of delighted contemplation, with all that is good and evil in it, so that we can almost understand the saying that Hector died and Troy fell that they might turn into a song. The difference between the world of imagination and the world of applied science, in which we actually spend our lives, is so great that the one can hardly understand the other. Applied science shows us a world of consistent, mechanical progress. There machines give birth to ever new generations of machines; but the point to be observed is that the new machines are always an improvement on the old, and begin where the old left off. If we attribute sentience to the new machine, we shall find that it simply does not understand the old; it is far ahead, in another world. But in the world of imagination and of human beings all is different. There you find no consistent progress, no starting where the previous generation left off; instead there is continuity. Every human being begins at the beginning, as his fathers did, with the same difficulties and pleasures, the same temptations, the same problem of good and evil, the same inward conflict, the same need to learn how to live, the same need to ask what life means. Conspicuous virtue, when he encounters it, may move him, or a new and saving faith; since the desire for goodness and truth is also in his nature. He will pass through the ancestral pattern, from birth to childhood and youth and manhood and age and death. He will feel hope and fear and love and hate and perhaps forgiveness. All this may seem dull and monotonous to the detached thinker, but it enchants the imagination for it is the image of all human life. But when change becomes too rapid, and the world around us alters from year to year, the ancestral image grows more indistinct than it was in simpler times, and the imagination cannot pierce to it as easily as it once could.

There has been change, of course, since the beginning of things. There have been crises and revolutions in the slow development of civilization in the past. Certain generations then probably found it hard to adapt themselves to some new invention, such as the use of iron instead of stone, or the discovery of agriculture fixing the nomad to one place, or the construction of great cities, or the consolidation of elaborate states, bringing new and difficult laws. But the change was different from change as we know it in our time, both in its speed and in its nature. It was brought about by a sort of rule of thumb, as when some farmer, having watched the behavior of nature, assisted it by planting seed in the uncovered soil; after that it was only a long step to the mattock and the plow. These changes soon appeared natural to the ordinary man and were absorbed into his life. But the great changes in modern life have been produced by means which the ordinary man does not understand. The modern workman does not know his world as the plowman once did; sometimes he does not even understand what his hands are doing. There is a gap between him and the world which his work perpetuates, between the workman and the man himself, so that it is not easy for imagination to see through the one to the other.

This is one of the reasons why some poets are so concerned with the problem of being contemporary; they feel that the world in which they live is unlike any other with which poetry has ever dealt. The problem is a real one, and the best statement of it I know of is in an essay by Stephen Spender called "Inside the Cage" in his critical volume, *The Making of a Poem*. Being in the cage really means being enclosed in the contemporary world, without any outlet except into a future very like but worse than the present. The cage exists, and we live in it. Yet the imagination does not live entirely in it, but in thirty centuries at least, and beyond them in the ever deepening past which archaeology is excavating. We are here, and Homer and his lost ancestors are far away. Yet on the other hand we are human beings like the men and women in Homer. We are bound to the past generations by the same bond as to our neighbors, and if only for the sake of preserving the identity of mankind we must cherish memory. This means that how we regard the past is very important. Mr. Spender, speaking of the

kind of analysis which interprets the past and its works
in terms of the present, says:

The dead and their works should be regarded not as
illustrations of the ideology of the living but as coherent
indissoluble unities situated in past time. The sun and moon,
like Dante and Shakespeare, are far removed in time when
their light reaches us, but we do not, for that reason, con-
sider that the principles according to which they exist are
"historically correct for their time," though not for ours. . . .
The organised realities in Dante and Shakespeare do not
lead up to our contemporary development, they look at it
and criticise it. All co-exist. But in order to understand this
we have to see the reality of the dead as in some way ab-
solute in itself, and impossible to dissolve into our ideas
unless we are to be imprisoned in our own present. To talk
about "the suspension of disbelief" in approaching the faiths
of the past, already betrays the analytic attitude which
attempts to convert past beliefs into *our* ideas, and then
finds them unacceptable. We have to accept that past belief
was a fact, like a rock. And probably what is required of us
today is something far more complex than the so-called
complexities of analysis; we need both to employ the analytic
method and to reject it. To analyse the work, and to realise
at the same time that it maintains its own intrinsic reality,
like sun and moon, outside the analysis. What matters is
contact with the dead and their works as existent — coexist-
ent — fact, outside any attempt to resolve them into our
ideas.

Mr. Spender, I think, has the Marxian theory in mind
in what he says, and, perhaps, though it is so far removed
from Marx, the new criticism as well. He says of the one:
"No system which insists on analysing all pasts and

presents outside itself into its own ideology can co-exist with any other present or past." And he goes on: "However, even without Marxism, the co-existence which is talked of so glibly today, is in fact almost an unattainable ideal. Through the excessive practice of analytic methods and the widespread belief that analysis of the fact is more significant than the fact itself, every country, every culture, every school of thought has become isolated within its own terms."

The past is a living past, and past and present coexist: that also the imagination tells us. It opens the past to us as part of our own life, a vast extension of our present. It cannot admit that anything that ever happened among the dead is dead for us, or that all that men and women have done and suffered was merely meant to bring us where we are.

Yet, in spite of all that the past means for us, and although it remains so obstinately alive in the imagination, the remedy is not to keep living in it and turn away from the present. The acceptance of the past can enlarge and purify our image of human life; and Dante and Shakespeare do look at and criticize our age. But they did not know our age; they only knew something that is true of life in any age. Our contemporary life also asks to be interpreted in poetry, and, because it is so unlike that of any former age, has a peculiar need for those who can imaginatively interpret it. I have said a great deal about the present difficulties of poetry, and have tried to explain some of them, hoping that explanation may be of some use. I have spoken of the enigma of the public, and the ascendency of criticism, and science, and the effect on the imagination of a world becoming more and more a world of secondary objects. I have also tried to give an idea of the virtue of the poetic imagination, its ancient succession, and the urgent need for it in our time. Poetry in any age is bound to be contemporary. What I have tried to urge is that poetry will not truly be contemporary, or truly poetry, if it deals merely with the immediately perceived contemporary world as if that existed by itself and were isolated from all that preceded it. As it is, our age offers opportunities for the imagination as well as difficulties: anthropology and archaeology have extended the possible world of imagination in time, while psychology has explored the regions of the unconscious. It is the contemporary world itself which presents us with these new provinces accessible to the imagination, and the poet is free to use them for his own purposes, though he will not, of course, use them in the same way as the archaeologist and the psychologist. The categories of psychology will probably be of little use to him, and may do him harm; but the dream life of the unconscious with its own image of life is certain some time to enter into and deepen the archetypal images of the imagination. I mean the actual dream life, not the daydream or the decorative fantasy. There is this vast background of existence only guessed at in past poetry at moments when it did not quite know what it was doing. Perhaps in that obscure region we still exist timelessly, though we may be lying asleep in a modern bed in the modern world.

The relation between time past, time present, and time future is always with us, and we are reminded of it in T. S. Eliot's poem "Four Quartets." Our world presents the imagination with certain questions not asked before, or not asked in the same way. Public indifference may be expected to continue, but perhaps the audience will increase when poetry loses what obscurity is left in it by attempting greater themes, for great themes have to be stated clearly. A great theme greatly treated might still put poetry back in its old place.

THE PUBLIC AND THE POET

I have been trying to measure the gap between the public and the poet, and to find some explanation why it is so great. I began with the time when there was neither poet nor public, when the anonymous song or ballad was transmitted from generation to generation by the peasantry, and poetry was a possession so common that poet and audience were lost in it, indistinguishably. That estate has gone long since and cannot be recovered; we cannot even wish for it; we have been irreversibly changed. At best we can gain from that oral poetry the beauty which is in it, and the knowledge that poetry is not a thing reserved for a few, since it was once, and for a long time, treasured and fostered by so many. If, knowing this, we could be brought to modify our contemporary notion of poetry as a rarified and special and often difficult thing, it might have a salutary effect on our criticism and our practice of poetry as well.

94

The difficulty is that the general neglect of poetry is as much a public as a literary question, and has the shifting, provisional quality of the questions we read about in the newspapers, where there is, on the one hand, a little evidence, a glaring fact or two, in a great vacuum; and, on the other, our insufficient knowledge and our fallible worldly wisdom. Looking at the relation between the poet and the public, we find that one of these, the poet, is quite definite, and the other, the public, so vague that we cannot present it to ourselves in any form, or even imagine it. In this world we know people; we see them perpetually, and, knowing them, we can imagine people we have never seen. We do this every now and then; the poet and the novelist do it habitually. But, when we try to imagine the public, and to see it in these human terms, it remains anonymous and invisible, as if it lived in a time and space of its own. It seems to be contemporary and nothing but contemporary, to exist somehow in the endless repetition of the moment. It is insubstantial, almost ghostly. Kierkegaard, who wrote about it a hundred years ago, was impressed then by this curious difficulty in laying hold of it. "Years might be spent," he said, "gathering the public together, and still it would not be there." He was outraged by its fickleness. "If a man adopts public opinion today and is hissed tomorrow, he is hissed by the public." He himself had been jeered at and humiliated by the public of Copenhagen, and he wrote with feeling.

If we try, then, to seize the public imaginatively, and

poetry cannot help doing that, we are faced with a sequence of impossibilities. We learn all we know about the human passions and affections from people we know and from ourselves, from nature, history, imaginative literature, philosophy, religion, and other records of human life that have come down to us. These do not tell us much about the public, and the public itself tells us nothing; when it speaks to us it speaks indirectly, at intervals, in an ambiguous voice, in newspapers. What we do discover about it seems very strange. Apparently it has not been born and will not die, has no childhood or youth or middle or old age. It does not fall in or out of love, is neither married nor single, and is exempt from happiness and grief. It seems to be an impersonal something, a collectivity which, if you break it up, does not reduce itself to a single human being, but at best into chunks of itself, sections, percentages. One might be tempted, after this, to regard it as a purely statistical entity; yet strangely enough it has opinions and feelings, though of a very general kind. There is something called public approval, and something called public disapproval. There is public interest and public apathy. And there is, at rare moments, public fury, which can be dangerous.

In spite of this, to continue the imaginative picture, the public seems to be a stabilizing element in society; it has the advantage of being everybody. It unites us, but at the same time it has a providential safeguard, that of being divided in an orderly way within itself; and, from this, according to political theorists, comes the possibility of progress. The Republican and the Democrat in the United States, the Conservative and the Labourite in Britain, read their morning newspaper on the same train, but read it against each other, with mild elation or mild dejection. Their emotions may be quite warm as they sit there; since it is hard for anyone even faintly interested in politics to read the news quite through without some passing irritation. Yet, though the public is divided within itself, the division in any moderately freely run country is seldom fatally embittered; for a free public has a fairly steady prejudice in favor of humanity. This need not keep it from being very changeable, as politicians complain, and it can displace one political party and install the opposing one in the course of a few years. Kierkegaard, remembering the insults he had endured, says of the public which sneered at his physical defects: "That indolent mass sits with its legs crossed wearing an air of superiority, and anyone who tries to work, whether king, official, schoolteacher or the better type of journalist, the poet or the artist, has to struggle to drag the public along with it, while the public thinks in its own superior way that it is the horse." Since then things have changed. Whatever the public may have been in Kierkegaard's time, we cannot think of it now as sitting, cross-legged, with an air of superiority; we think of it rather as gazing up with a beseeching look at those who really know; for the great ascendency of science has brought a superstitious reverence for authority, the authority of those who are in the secret.

Kierkegaard has one observation in particular which brings us nearer to the mystery of the public. "A public," he says, "is neither a nation, nor a generation, nor a community, nor a society, nor these particular men, for all these are only what they are through the concrete." (I think by the concrete is meant something with a history and a development, an organic life.) "No single person who belongs to the public makes a real commitment; for some hours of the day, perhaps, he belongs to the public — at moments when he is nothing else, since when he really is what he is, he does not form part of the public. Made up of such individuals, of individuals at the moments when they are nothing, a public is a kind of gigantic something, an abstract and deserted void which is everything and nothing." He decides at last that this "abstract whole" is "formed in the most ludicrous way, by all participants becoming a third party (an onlooker)."

It is hard to separate the truth from the spleen in these words. The public is certainly not made up "of individuals at the moments when they are nothing," and it is not formed "by all participants becoming a third party (an onlooker)." There is some truth in this generalization; the public does contain a great number of third parties, and of onlookers, and a great number whose response to public questions is so vague as to amount

almost to nothing. But there are also a number of respon-
sible people really concerned with public things, and
reformers trying to drag the rest of the public along with
them. These are not members of the public merely when,
as Kierkegaard says, they have nothing else to do, and to
him they may not belong to the public at all. But in the
crises of society our liberties may depend upon them.

The public, then, is such an amorphous body that it is
impossible to make it quite real to ourselves. Kierkegaard
does tell us something about it when he says that it is
that part of us, or those hours in our life, which we give
to public things, forgetting our own. Insofar as we do
that, and all of us do it, we belong, however slightly, to
the public. Perhaps the best way to regard the public is
as a mental state shared by us all for a smaller or greater
part of our lives, rather than as the multitude of human
beings summoned up by the imagination, with all the
feelings and thoughts and difficulties and frustrations
and joys and griefs which human beings are subject to.
The public is simple and impersonal. It is confined to
general problems and ideas. In its sphere it has no need
to encounter the intimate impact of things, and it has no
technique for doing so. When its sphere is artificially
expanded — as it has been, for instance, in Communist
countries — and every question becomes a public ques-
tion, and all one thinks and does must be done for the
collectivity, and one's most intimate feelings are manipu-
lated, until the living together of a couple in marriage
and the bringing up of their children are regarded as

public duties, and human beings have no life of their own, the public really becomes what Kierkegaard calls a "gigantic something, an abstract and deserted void which is everything and nothing." But, in its normal working in democratic countries (and it was democracy that created it) the public obviously has an indispensable function. It can sometimes become a tyranny, but then it has within itself the power to protest that it has become a tyranny and to struggle to extricate itself.

Let us think of the public, then, as that part of us or those hours in our lives which we give, idly or seriously, to public and general things. Obviously the hours and the attention we give to these things are far greater now than they were in the past. Consider the fears of Wordsworth a hundred years ago, when newspapers were still in their infancy, and the radio and television were unknown. He complained that the increasing accumulation in towns, the report of great public events, the rapid communication of information, leading to a degrading thirst after outrageous stimulants, had blunted the discriminating powers of the mind and reduced it to a state of almost savage torpor. That "degrading thirst after outrageous stimulation," he goes on to say, makes him "almost ashamed to have spoken of the feeble endeavour made in these volumes [the two volumes of the *Lyrical Ballads*] to counteract it."

The time spent over "the rapid communication of information" must have been relatively small in Wordsworth's day, and the number of people who read the

news even smaller. Now the news is read or heard or
seen by everybody, and the time spent upon it through
all these means is considerable. We are the public while
we read and listen and look on, and perhaps for a little
longer, if we think about what we have read or heard or
seen. Could we keep in some special insulated compart-
ment of ourselves these minutes or hours which we
daily spend in this way, there would be no need to speak
with concern of them or of their relation to poetry. But
we are not constituted in that way; whatever we do or
whatever is done to us goes into our experience. Things
which take up little time but are repeated day after day
— the morning exercise, the ten minutes spent on Yoga,
the half-hour spent on the newspaper — have a total
effect upon us, not merely the specific effect for which
they are intended. There have been intense experiences,
lasting only a few minutes, which have changed men's
lives. The effect of the newspaper, the wireless, and tele-
vision is rarely intense, but it is regular and it has changed
the quality of our experience. Perhaps its main effect,
apart from merely distracting us, is to give our minds
and feelings a certain predilection for the abstract and
the cliché; and the cliché is the popular expression of the
abstract. It tends to make us view life impersonally, as
third parties and onlookers, and it inclines us to use, even
when we are strongly moved, a kind of language which
is suited only for general ideas and newspaper reports, or
even for headlines. The public, which has its genuine
function, in this way insinuates itself into our private

lives. And that is a matter of importance, for the language we use colors and circumscribes our feelings, our thoughts, and our image of the world.

Returning to the poet, the idea of confronting him with the public, if this is what it is, appears strangely anomalous. He cannot speak its language, which is the language of the third party and the onlooker. He abhors the cliché. He is not concerned with life in its generality, but in its immediacy and its individuality. His object is to see into the life of people, to enter into their feelings and thoughts, good and bad. What can he say to the public, or the public to him? The public seems to be designed for one purpose and the poet for another.

The public, as Kierkegaard described it, is a comparatively new thing. It was made possible by general education. A public must be able to read; that is the only way in which it can become conscious of itself. The old ballads were the poetry of those who could not read. They are in the same world as those medieval churches where the frescoed walls are a picture book of the Bible story, intended for everyone, the lettered and the unlettered, designed to delight the one and to delight and instruct the other. We step into the picture book when we enter a church with frescoes picturing the Creation, the history of the patriarchs and the Judaean kings and prophets, the Annunciation, the birth, life, and death of Christ, and the wanderings of the apostles. God in the height, the story of His chosen people, the coming of the Redeemer; all are there, and many of the pictured episodes were recognized by the ignorant peasant five centuries ago which may puzzle a well-read onlooker today. For centuries the story and the painting and the poetry were shared by all, from the different orders of society. The story in the ballads was not the story we see on the walls of the church of Mon Reale in Sicily; it was a purely human story, partly Christian and partly pagan; but this was the world in which it could continue to exist.

There has been also, since quite early in the Middle Ages, a poetry for the few; for lack of a better term I shall call it court poetry, since it was mainly fostered in the courts of kings and princes. It attempted things far beyond the reach of the folk song and ballad, and the world in which it moved would have been incomprehensible to the peasantry. It was addressed to a cultivated audience, aware of the world of Greece and Rome, and acquainted with the classical heroes and gods and goddesses. The ballads are sunk just as deep in time, but what they show us are the Daemon Lover and the Queen of Elfland, not Achilles or Venus. The poetry of the courts was aware of itself as an art, as folk poetry was not; poets set themselves to develop all the resources that language and measure and rhyme afforded them, inventing and elaborating new forms, their minds already fixed on poetry as the main thing, and only after that on their audience. English poetry ever since Chaucer has followed that model.

The new poet did not shrink from the risk of being

obscure. In *La Vita Nuova* and the *Convivio* Dante takes
the danger for granted and sets out to explain himself
to his reader. In *La Vita Nuova* he describes the occasion
of his poems to Beatrice, and how they came to be
written, and in the *Convivio* he lays down the rules by
which the sacred poems in that book are to be inter-
preted. They are to be interpreted in two or three or four
ways: the literal, the allegorical, the moral, and the ana-
gogical. He confesses that the poems he is considering
"are scarcely intelligible without a literal and anagogical
commentary," and "invites those who are too busy or
too slothful to study for themselves (but not those who
are too vicious or too incompetent) to come and share
the intellectual feast." He is thinking of an audience able
to recognize the secret as well as the open meanings in
the poems. The interpretation he employs is not merely
literal or verbal, as it is in contemporary criticism; for
the poems have a further meaning behind the literal one
which is also to be interpreted, and sometimes beyond
that a third and a fourth. He treats in these poems of the
mystery of the divine wisdom, "the brightness of the
eternal light, the spotless mirror of the majesty of God."
The reach of such poetry is far beyond that of the
ballads.

Dante stands by himself, and what I have called court
poetry rarely attempted themes so great as this, and,
except in the works of the metaphysical and mystical
poets, was concerned with this world. The peasantry
were quite unaware of the court poets and the poetry

that celebrated their world, and in this fortunate blindness lay their safety: the spoken ballads could still perpetuate themselves in their own place. Yet the Elizabethan court poets seem to have known the folksinger as a friendly neighbor, and Sir Philip Sidney writes with admiration of the fine ballad of Chevy Chase. The poetry of the people and that of the few lived side by side for a while in a friendly parallel, the public being still nonexistent.

Apart from these two kinds of poetry, in the time of Elizabeth and James there was the poetic play as well. The morality and the miracle play were the public entertainment of the Middle Ages; in the Elizabethan age the play became the vehicle of great poetry, and it cut across the other two poetic modes to reach a general audience. That age did not last long, but, when it was at its height, three modes of poetry existed together, two with a special audience of their own, and the third with an audience drawn from the other two. This position was very different from ours. It was made possible by an order very unlike ours, and the acceptance of that order. Faced with the public we have our own classifications to indicate the differences in quality: such half-derogatory terms as low-brow and middle-brow and high-brow. But these do not correspond to the old categories, for folk poetry was not low-brow and court poetry was only now and then high-brow. These modern distinctions in their rough and ready way are intended as intellectual distinctions; the older distinction expressed rather a difference in sensibility and knowledge and position for which we have no convenient cliché. The earlier arrangement had the great advantage from the poet's point of view that he knew his audience, and could speak to it without further thought. Now, confronted with an undifferentiated public, the poet does not know to whom he is speaking.

So much for the public, which is only a part of the problem. The poet cannot win now the same position with the public as the folk singer and the court poet enjoyed with their separate audiences, for the public is both there and not there. So, although he may long to become a popular poet, he cannot. And the attempt, if he tried, would only degrade poetry, without being of any profit to the public. I read recently, in a bulletin of the Committee of Science and Freedom, a dialogue between Dr. Weyman-Weghe and Professor Josef Pieper of Münster University. Certain things which Professor Pieper says about science and philosophy there have a bearing on poetry. "Man is a being," he says, "whose essential nature is the desire to see and know — so much so that his ultimate realisation in eternal life is designated with the term *visio beatifica*. In the activity of seeing and understanding, man is doing what, essentially, he wants to do; and in the act of knowing he is truly free."

Professor Pieper goes on:

To this formulation one must immediately add the qualification that this "knowing" which is said to set man free is not directed towards any concrete set of phenomena in the

outside world but towards reality as a whole, and its ulti-
mate significance. The proposition should therefore read:
in perceiving and grasping the ultimate nature of reality as
a whole, man is doing what he really wants to do, and in
so far as he does this, he is free. This knowledge, of which
the essence is that it is "non-practical" and therefore does
not "serve" any external criterion, is the only knowledge
that is free, and it gives freedom to mankind. One may say
therefore, that this kind of knowledge is free and has the
power to make us free . . . because it is not directed towards
the realisation of concrete aims but towards the discovery
of truth. And it is the truth that sets us free — not any
particular truth but the whole truth.

Professor Pieper is asserting the real freedom of science
and of all thinking against a philosophy which he traces
back to Descartes, a practical philosophy whose object
was to make us "masters and owners of nature." He finds
its latest expression in the frank attitude of totalitarian
states where, "science has reached the position where it
must constantly answer the question: 'What contribution
does this make to the Five Years Plan?'" Man's essential
desire, "to see and to know," which is the mainspring of
science, is ignored when science becomes "an intellectual
industry," and at the same time science, in disregarding
its true end, loses its freedom and with that its meaning.
The object of knowledge is not power, Jacques Maritain
has pointed out; the object of knowledge is truth.

Poetry too has its object, which is not knowledge in the
scientific or philosophical sense, but the creation of a true
image of life. We all help to create that image, for

imagination is a faculty as natural to us as the desire to see and to know; it is the most common form of the same faculty. Without it we would not understand one another, or make friends, or fall in love, or know what love and friendship and life are. The supreme expression of imagination is in poetry, and so like philosophy and science it has a responsibility to itself: the responsibility to preserve a true image of life. If the image is true, poetry fulfills its end. Anything that distorts the image, any tendency to oversimplify or soften it so that it may be more acceptable to a greater number of people, falsifies it, degrades those for whom it is intended, and cannot set us free. This means that the first allegiance of any poet is to imaginative truth, and that if he is to serve mankind, that is the only way in which he can do it.

But it does not mean that he should turn inward into the complex problems of poetry, or be concerned with poetry as a problem. That is something which has commonly happened in the last fifty years. There was some excuse for it after the years of experiment associated with Mr. Eliot and Mr. Pound. To them, about 1910, poetry seemed to have come to a dead end, and intense thought had to be given to it. The experiments of that time and the succeeding years have become a part of literary history. As they were new and strange when they were first attempted, they were found difficult by the reader; and they seem to have left for a time in the minds of poets and critics the belief that poetry should be difficult. The experimenters have done their work, and we should be thankful to them. There have been many experimenters in English poetry: Chaucer was one; and Spenser, Milton, Dryden, and Wordsworth were all experimenters. The experimenters of forty years ago did something to poetry and something for poetry. One kind of poetry was written before T. S. Eliot, and another kind after him. But the point of an experiment is that it should solve the particular problem set for it. This was done in the twenties. Yet in spite of that there is a mild outcry against young poets because they do not go on experimenting; it comes mainly from people who remember the excitements of the twenties, a great age, as Wyndham Lewis called it, that did not come off. Yet, if we think of the remaining half of this century as running on without cessation from experiment to experiment, with not even a decade's length of easy speech, the prospect is alarming. So far as I can judge their work, young poets now find themselves free to write in a natural tongue. What their mentors do not realize is that to write naturally, especially in verse, is one of the most difficult things in the world; naturalness does not come easily to the awkward human race, and is an achievement of art.

There remains the temptation for poets to turn inward into poetry, to lock themselves into a hygienic prison where they speak only to one another, and to the critic, their stern warder. In the end a poet must create his audience, and to do that he must turn outward. Even if he is conscious of having no audience, he must imagine one. That may be the way to conjure it out of the public void. Yeats, who had to wait for it long, declared that you must have an audience, and that he could not write without one. Anyone reading his poetry must feel that his audience was an imaginary one long before it became real. To imagine an audience, one must hold up before himself the variety of human life, for from that diversity the audience will be drawn. The poet need not think of the public — its vastness and impersonality would daunt anyone; he should reflect instead that in no other age than ours — I mean the last hundred years or so — has a poet had to deal with it. He has to see past it, or through it, to the men and women, with their individual lives, who in some strange way and without their choice are part of it, and yet are hidden by it.

✤ ✤ ✤

A NOTE ON SOURCES

To assist the reader in locating the quotations used by Edwin Muir, the following list has been compiled.

PAGES

4–5, 6, 30   William Wordsworth. Preface to the Second Edition (1800), *Lyrical Ballads.*

7   Samuel Taylor Coleridge. "Dejection: An Ode," lines 51–52.

13   Robert Burns. "Epistle to Davie, a Brother Poet," stanza 5; "To a Mouse," stanza 7.
(Versions of the following anonymous ballads vary. Some may be found in the *Oxford Book of English Verse* [Oxford, 1939], and the *Oxford Book of Ballads* [Oxford, 1910], both edited by Arthur Quiller-Couch.)

14   Anonymous. "Clerk Saunders," stanza 1; "The Queen's Marie," stanza 19.

14, 18, 19   Anonymous. "Sir Patrick Spens," part I, stanza 1; part II, stanzas 7, 9, 10, 11.

SOURCES

14   Anonymous. "The Daemon Lover."

16–17, 21   Anonymous. "Thomas the Rhymer," stanzas 11, 12, 13, 15, 2.

17   Anonymous. "Fairy's Song."

20   Anonymous. "Waly, Waly."

21   Anonymous. "The Twa Sisters."

25, 26   Plato. "Ion," translated by Percy Bysshe Shelley.

31, 32–33   Wordsworth. "The Affliction of Margaret."

34, 36   Wordsworth. "Lines composed a few miles above Tintern Abbey."

35   Wordsworth. "Extempore Effusion Upon the Death of James Hogg."

37   Wordsworth. "Ode. Intimations of Immortality."

38   Wordsworth. "Three Years She Grew in Sun and Shower."

39, 40   Wordsworth. "The Prelude."

43   Yeats. "The Song of the Happy Shepherd."

45   Yeats. "Ephemera."

46   Yeats. "The Rose of the World."
(Unless otherwise indicated, quotations from W. B. Yeats are from *The Collected Poems of W. B. Yeats*, Definitive Edition © The Macmillan Company 1956. Used by permission of The Macmillan Company, New York; Macmillan & Co. Ltd., London; and Mrs. W. B. Yeats.)

46–47   William Morris. "Golden Wings."

48   Yeats. Controversy with John Eglinton in *The Dublin Daily Express*; Y. K. Narayana Menon, *The Development of William Butler Yeats* (Edinburgh, 1942), p. 37.

48   Yeats to AE. April 1904. *Letters of W. B. Yeats*, ed. Allan Wade (New York, 1955), pp. 433–434.

49   Yeats. "The Tree of Life," quoted by Menon, p. 38.

SOURCES

50   Yeats to Mrs. Shakespear. 27 February 1934. *Letters,* p. 300.

51   Yeats. "Among School Children."

52–53   Yeats. "Remorse for Intemperate Speech."

53   Yeats. *The Observer,* 21 January 1917.

54   Yeats. "The Tragic Generation," *The Autobiography of William Butler Yeats* (New York, 1953), p. 169.

55   Yeats. "Adam's Curse"; "September 1913."

56   Yeats. "Easter 1916."

56–57   Yeats. "A Prayer for My Daughter."

57   Yeats. "A Dialogue of Self and Soul"; "His Phoenix"; "Vacillation."

58   Yeats. "In Memory of Major Robert Gregory"; "Running to Paradise."

59   Yeats. "Crazy Jane on God"; "Tom the Lunatic"; "The Delphic Oracle upon Plotinus."

60   Yeats to Lady Dorothy Wellesley. April 1936. *Letters on Poetry from W. B. Yeats to Dorothy Wellesley* (New York, London, 1940), p. 64.

64–65   William Empson. *Seven Types of Ambiguity* (New York, 1955), pp. 2–3.

67–68, 75   Cleanth Brooks. "The Motivation of Tennyson's Weeper," *The Well Wrought Urn* (New York, 1947), pp. 153–154.

73   Harold Osborne. *Aesthetics and Criticism* (London, 1955).

95, 97–98, 100   Soren Kierkegaard. "The Individual and the Public," *A Kierkegaard Anthology,* ed. Robert Bretall (Prineton, 1946), pp. 265–266, 266–267.

100   Wordsworth. Preface, *Lyrical Ballads.*

104   Dante. *Convivio,* First Treatise, Introductory Note.

INDEX OF NAMES

INDEX

ABOUT THE AUTHOR

Edwin Muir (1887-1959) was born in Deerness, Orkney Island, Scotland, to a tenant farmer. While in his mid-teens Muir and his family were forced to leave the Orkneys and move to Glasgow. This move, coupled with the ensuing deaths of his parents and two of his brothers, led Muir to undergo psychoanalysis. T.S. Eliot called Muir's poetry remarkable and said he "will remain among the poets who have added glory to the English language." Muir was a well-respected literary critic and co-translator with his wife of the works of Franz Kafka.

THE GRAYWOLF
DISCOVERY SERIES

BEYOND THE MOUNTAIN
by Elizabeth Arthur

STILL LIFE WITH INSECTS
by Brian Kiteley